FOREIGN STUDENTS

AND HIGHER EDUCATION

IN THE UNITED STATES

Studies in
Universities and World Affairs —

AMERICAN COLLEGE LIFE AS EDUCATION IN WORLD OUTLOOK
Howard E. Wilson

FOREIGN STUDENTS AND HIGHER EDUCATION
IN THE UNITED STATES
Cora Du Bois

WORLD AFFAIRS AND THE COLLEGE CURRICULUM
Vincent Baker

TRAINING OF SPECIALISTS IN INTERNATIONAL RELATIONS
C. Dale Fuller

UNIVERSITY RESEARCH ON WORLD AFFAIRS
John Gange

THE UNIVERSITY, THE CITIZEN, AND WORLD AFFAIRS
Cyril O. Houle and Charles A. Nelson

WORLD AFFAIRS IN INSTITUTIONS OF HIGHER EDUCATION
IN THE SOUTH
Fred Cole and Richard W. Sterling

AMERICAN UNIVERSITIES IN WORLD AFFAIRS:
A GENERAL REPORT
Howard E. Wilson

FOREIGN STUDENTS

AND HIGHER EDUCATION

IN THE UNITED STATES

22181

CORA DU BOIS

Zemurray Professor

Harvard University–Radcliffe College

AMERICAN COUNCIL ON EDUCATION • *Washington, D. C.*

Prepared for the Carnegie Endowment for International Peace and the Institute of International Education; published by the American Council on Education

FOREWORD

The Carnegie Endowment for International Peace and the Institute of International Education have jointly sponsored this review of the program for foreign students in the colleges and universities of the United States. It is the latest manifestation of the community of interests of the two organizations, which have worked together informally for more than thirty years. The Institute's concern with international exchange programs of high quality is naturally related closely to the Endowment's interest in broad problems of international affairs.

Dr. Du Bois brings to this study a unique background. Her training and insight in anthropology and psychiatry and her extensive experiences in Europe and Asia in themselves well qualify her to look critically at this field. In addition, Dr. Du Bois, as former research director of the Institute of International Education, has had the opportunity to observe the operations of exchange programs as they affect individual participants, educational institutions, and the numerous agencies, both public and private, which operate in this area.

Exchange of persons is now an accepted and vital part of both the educational and foreign affairs pattern of the United States. We believe that Dr. Du Bois' incisive analyses of the status, potentialities, and problems in this constantly evolving field will contribute much to better understanding of international educational exchange.

> Joseph E. Johnson, *President*
> *Carnegie Endowment for International Peace*
>
> Kenneth Holland, *President*
> *Institute of International Education*

v

EDITOR'S FOREWORD

I$_N$ 1950 the Carnegie Endowment for International Peace began a program of studies focused on the relation of American universities to world affairs. Eight institutions of higher education cooperated with the Endowment in exploratory surveys of their resources and activities bearing on international relations. The results of their exploration were reported in a small volume on *Universities and World Affairs* published in 1951.[1]

The report stressed the fact that the modern university's relation to world affairs is not limited to the formal teaching of international relations. In addition to providing instruction, both for the general student and for specialists-to-be, a college or university has heavy and complex responsibilities for advancing research bearing on the conduct of international relations. Campus voices have strong influence in adult education about world affairs, and universities conduct consequential programs reaching large off-campus audiences. American students demonstrate their concern with world matters in extracurricular activities and in foreign travel—in connection with military service or in connection with "study tours." And American institutions of higher education have, particularly since World War II, become focal centers in the interchange of persons across national boundary lines. The arrival of great numbers of foreign students and professors is an outstanding phenomenon in the relationship of American universities to the contemporary American situation in world affairs.

Following publication in 1951 of the Endowment's intro-

[1] Howard E. Wilson, *Universities and World Affairs* (New York: Carnegie Endowment for International Peace, 1951).

ductory handbook on *Universities and World Affairs* and presentation of the report in a series of regional conferences, a widely representative group of colleges and universities undertook to make self-surveys and appraisals of their resources, activities, and responsibilities respecting foreign relations and international affairs. Since that time sixty institutions have completed surveys which were mimeographed for distribution among the cooperating group.

All the reports from these colleges and universities, as well as many related studies conducted under other auspices, indicate the importance of a comprehensive, coordinated approach to analysis of the interrelations between universities and world affairs. The reports provide evidence that colleges and universities have undertaken almost haphazardly many enterprises involving instruction or research or student life as related to international interests. There is need for stock-taking, for more thoughtful conservation of educational resources, for appraisal by each institution of what it can most successfully and wisely continue to do in view of the rising importance of world affairs. Nowhere is this need more apparent than in the policies and practices by which we receive foreign students.

As an outgrowth of the Carnegie Endowment's program of studies on universities and world affairs, a series of topical volumes, of which this is one, are in process of publication by the American Council on Education. The full list of titles in the series appears on page ii of the present volume. The volumes draw heavily on the survey experiences in cooperating colleges and universities, but are not limited to that experience. They deal with matters revealed as consequential in the surveys, and, in dealing with those matters, draw on all available sources of information.

This volume on *Foreign Students and Higher Education in the United States* is presented by the Endowment in cooperation with the Institute of International Education. Dr. Du Bois, formerly director of research for the Institute and now on the faculty of Harvard University, analyzes, with the insight of an anthropologist, the sojourn of foreign students in American colleges and universities. In her presentation she draws heavily on the researches in this area which have been undertaken in recent years by the Social Science Research Council. Her analyses and findings are of consequence to all who deal with foreign students, or who formulate policies affecting foreign students in America. It is the hope and the expectation of the Endowment and the Institute, as well as the publishers, that the volume will be useful in aiding colleges and universities to deal with the obligations and opportunities presented to the United States by the arrival of foreign students from all the world.

HOWARD E. WILSON

August 1, 1955

PREFACE

THE SUBJECT of foreign students is of wide interest in this country—and at the same time it is a subject about which there are striking gaps in our knowledge. This volume attempts to add to the increasing, but insufficient, information and still inadequate formulations available.

This volume is an outgrowth of the survey of American universities and world affairs, stimulated and sponsored by the Carnegie Endowment for International Peace. As such, the discussion centers on the university- and college-affiliated visitors from abroad who intend only a study sojourn in the United States. Foreigners studying in other nations and Americans who become foreign students in another country are included only to the degree that generalizations about cross-cultural education may be valid in a broad sense. Again, it would have been interesting to explore questions that concern, say, the teen-age and high school exchangees and the visiting leaders and trainees sponsored by various private associations and federal agencies, but the whole problem of cross-cultural adjustment is so extensive that no single volume or writer can be expected—or should try—to encompass it.

Even within the limited category of foreign students considered here, more questions will be raised than answered. However, a question well posed will often go far toward assuring an eventual answer; this is one of the tasks attempted here.

When the Carnegie Endowment suggested this volume, it was hoped that it would prove useful to educators, educational administrators, and educational counselors. For this reason the writer has attempted to keep practical issues in mind. The book is divided into three main parts: Part One is a brief and generalized presentation of the contemporary trends with respect to study abroad; Part Two stresses some of the psychological and sociological factors that affect foreign students from the time they plan their foreign study sojourn until they return home; Part Three is addressed to the role that American educational institutions can, or do, play with respect to foreign students. The book is not in the nature of a handbook, with the usual administrative categories and procedural steps. There is no intention of proceeding systematically through questions of selection, placement, academic credits, visas, orientation, financing and insurance, housing, and hospitality.

It is the writer's opinion that in the long run both the perspectives afforded by social science and a description and appraisal of ongoing practices are necessary to achieve operational and administrative effectiveness. Therefore, the aim here is to bring some of the ideas that stem from pure research to bear on practical problems—an approach that is consonant with the purposes of the Carnegie Endowment in sponsoring the over-all study.

For example, advancement in our knowledge about foreign students may be gained by considering the relationships between individual motivation and legislative goals, or by pondering the various types of learning congenial to different categories of students, or by speculating about how various types of individuals relate themselves to new situations. The customary administrative and operational steps constitute part of this "reality," and such procedures may be seen in a new and perhaps sharper light if they are placed in a different perspective.

This volume limits itself to the more intuitive procedures and attempts to offer insights rather than proof. Such an approach obviously risks offending both social scientists and those who work with foreign students. A volume which would begin with foreign students as individuals and systematically structure levels of generalization in the approved scientific fashion would be a welcome handbook, but neither the information nor the concepts available permit such a procedure to be pursued rigorously.

In any discussion of foreign students and foreign student programs a striking factor is the interest it engenders and the emotional involvement it stimulates. Community leaders, educators, and government officials meet in forums, committees, and conferences to exchange information and judgments that derive from their experience. The views they express are frequently buttressed by isolated and often unhappy anecdotes. For example, immigration regulations alone will precipitate long and complicated technical discussions. The diversity of both positive and negative generalizations about foreign students, as well as the high hopes expressed, suggest wishful thinking. If this volume can in some degree place the subject of study abroad in an appropriate perspective, the subject may then carry fewer unrealistic and disillusioning expectations.

For those interested in background material, a summary of quantitative and analytic materials available may be helpful.

An annual census of foreign students was conducted by the Committee on Friendly Relations Among Foreign Students beginning in 1915 and continuing until 1945, although for many years it was far from complete. Beginning in 1921 the Institute of International Education cooperated with the committee in circulating the census questionnaires, although the committee continued responsibility for tabulating the results.

In 1949 the Institute of International Education began publishing an annual census in *Education for One World*.[1] At that time the compilation was not conceived as a tool for investigations, as evidenced by the shift in categories from year to year;

[1] Beginning in 1954-55 the material reported by the Institute was broadened and the title of the report changed to *Open Doors: A Report on Three Surveys: Foreign Students, Foreign Faculty Members, Foreign Doctors in the United States, 1954–55.* (New York: The Institute, 1955).

thus, it may be used only for the broadest of comparisons.[2] Recently, however, the Institute, with support from the Ford Foundation, has established a central index into which are to be accumulated punch cards covering inbound and outbound exchangees for the last twenty-five years, and once this is done, the names of foreign students obtained annually will also be added. Originally the backlog was estimated at some 400,000 names, but a figure of 250,000 may be nearer the mark. This central index should in time become a valuable tool and an indispensable adjunct both to study and action in the field of American cross-cultural contacts.

Beginning in 1952 the United States Office of Education, acting primarily as an agent of the Department of State, has undertaken to list persons receiving government grants. This list includes names of persons granted Department of State awards and some of those who have received awards from the Foreign Operations Administration.[3]

Since 1948 UNESCO has published annually *Study Abroad*, an excellent compilation of quantitative and analytic materials. Each year's publication has proved increasingly useful.

In 1951, W. Rex Crawford and Margaret Van B. Cole undertook, under the auspices of the Social Science Research Council, the compilation of a bibliography on the exchange of persons and simultaneously prepared a paper entitled "Survey of the Exchange of Persons: The Present Situation." This project represents the most recent and by far the most complete effort in this direction. The bibliography runs to some forty-six typewritten pages and has not yet been reproduced for distribution, although a short, selected bibliography is available; the survey paper has been mimeographed.[4] The materials produced

---

[2] Cora Du Bois, "Research in Cross-Cultural Education," Institute of International Education *News Bulletin*, June 1953, p. 7.

[3] Oral communication from the U.S. Office of Education.

[4] The survey and the selected bibliography may be obtained from the Social Science Research Council, 230 Park Ave., New York City.

by Dr. Crawford and Miss Cole disclose the fact that there is a considerable quantity of materials—and activities—related to foreign students. At the same time their materials reveal that much of this literature is of an ephemeral and fragmentary nature and often of dubious value for research purposes.

Also in 1951 the Social Science Research Council received a generous grant from three foundations for research in the foreign student field. The council established a Committee on Cross-Cultural Education to plan and supervise a series of studies. Although this research is still going on, the results that have been made available during the first exploratory phase of research are drawn upon in what follows.

Meanwhile, the International Educational Exchange Service (IES) program of the United States Department of State spent in 1952–53 something under $100,000 in evaluating its exchange program. In 1953–54 it allocated some $33,000 to outside research contracts alone for the appraisal of its programs.

Other groups are also making investigations in the field of intercultural education, with somewhat more limited funds or other resources. Master's and Ph.D. theses, especially in schools of education, are increasingly addressed to problems in this area. Implicit in all the studies is the conviction of the need and possibility of sound investigations in this area and the growing interest in it.

A word about terms is in order. The term "exchange program" has gained wide currency to designate much cross-cultural education that is neither "exchange" in the strict sense of the word nor programmatic. There are, in fact, relatively few direct exchange programs. Notable exceptions are the International Farm Youth Program of the National 4-H Clubs, the teacher exchange under the Fulbright Act, and a few other comparable programs. Actual exchange of persons can probably never be arranged on a large scale, and cultural distance tends to diminish both the number and possibilities of exchanges. For example, it is easier to exchange British and American schoolteachers than to exchange Syrian and American schoolteachers. The term "exchange" has increasingly tended to be applied to exchange of information or views rather than of people. But even here one wonders how valid the term is as meaning equal give-and-take.

The term "program" should probably be reserved for either governmental or privately sponsored fellowship arrangements. About half the individuals studying abroad do so with financial support from both public and private sources, while the other half finance themselves from personal resources and on individual initiative.

Finally—and perhaps really a first question—Who is a foreign student? The precise definition "a nonnational" is far from perfect. Thus, a Canadian, who is a nonnational, is closer to an understanding of the United States than is a Puerto Rican student, who technically is a national. This is a point to be noted only; the real emphasis in this volume is on cross-cultural educational experience.

Acknowledgments

The writer could never have attempted this volume without the cordial cooperation and the insights that have been given her, for she is a newcomer in the field of cross-cultural education. The staffs of the Institute of International Education, the National Association of Foreign Student Advisers, the Committee on Friendly Relations Among Foreign Students, various International Houses, the Department of State's International Educational Exchange Service, and, of course, the Carnegie Endowment for International Peace have provided facilities to learn and have given unstintingly of their time, knowledge, and experience.

The staff of the Social Science Research Council, its Committee on Cross-Cultural Education, and the group of distinguished scientists who engaged in the first phase of the committee's research have been equally generous in permitting me to draw heavily on their findings and formulations. My greatest single debt is clearly to those colleagues. I must hasten, however, to assume full responsibility for the views expressed here and for the sometimes flighty extension of their cautious and scrupulously scientific approach.

In over two years of association with workers in this field the writer has obviously incurred debts to innumerable individuals who cannot be listed here and to whom full and adequate acknowledgment cannot be made personally.

A final word. The writing of this manuscript was completed in 1954. No attempt has been made to bring figures and references up to date.

CORA DU BOIS

Cambridge, Massachusetts
March 2, 1956

CONTENTS

APPENDIXES

PART ONE

The Changing Scene

THE PURSUIT of learning beyond the boundaries of one's own community, nation, or culture is as old as learning itself. It stems from the human capacity for curiosity and adventure. It reflects the ability of human beings to communicate with each other at varying levels and with varying sophistication across the barriers of social particularities.[1]

To put into perspective the widespread concern (which at times seems to border on anxiety) expressed in current years about "the problem of the foreign student," it is necessary to know something of the long history of educational exchange. Actually, perhaps 95 percent of the students from abroad do not encounter "problems" in any serious sense of the word. On the contrary, their experience is richly educational in formal as well as informal aspects. But in the minds of many people

---

[1] For a brief statement of historical perspective on the interchange of persons see chap. 1 of Guy S. Metraux, *Exchange of Persons: The Evolution of Cross-Cultural Education*, Social Science Research Council Pamphlet, No. 9 (New York: The Council, June 1952). See also William H. Allaway, "Exchange of Persons: A Historical Analysis" (MS); W. R. Wheeler, H. H. King, and A. B. Davidson (eds.), *The Foreign Student in America: A Study by the Commission on Survey of Foreign Students in the United States of America, under the Auspices of the Friendly Relations Committees of the Young Men's Christian Association and the Young Women's Christian Association* (New York: Association Press, 1925).

1

one disappointed and embittered student overbalances the influence of the many students who are well adjusted while in the United States and after their return home. For every student guest to be a balanced individual capable of extracting maximum advantages from a study tour abroad or for every student guest to encounter only constructive situations and insightful Americans would be a perfection unattainable.

Nevertheless, it behooves those concerned with exchange of persons to do all within their power to provide a flexible and constructive environment for student guests. This requires an understanding of complex factors that operate on many levels and in many contexts.

Chapter 1

QUANTITATIVE INCREASE IN STUDENT EXCHANGES

IN REVIEWING briefly here the quantitative changes in the foreign student population of the United States, the year 1930–31 has been selected for purposes of comparison with the 1952 and the 1953 census.[1] In 1930 the impact of the depression years had not yet made itself felt and therefore the comparisons are for more nearly "normal" years.

Three major points emerge from such comparisons. First, 9,643 foreign students were studying in this country in 1930. In 1953, the number had grown to 33,647. Even allowing for more complete returns in 1953 than in 1930, this represents a 300 percent increase. For approximately the same period the enrollment of American students in our colleges and universities increased only slightly more than 100 percent.[2]

[1] For figures in this section see Institute of International Education, *Education for One World, 1951–52* (New York: The Institute, March 1952), passim, and the same title for 1952–53. Since these publications do not present the same data consistently in successive years, it has been necessary to refer to two volumes for purposes of comparison.

[2] U.S. Office of Education orally gave the following figures: for the academic year 1929–30, the college and university enrollment in the United States was 1,100,737; for 1951–52, the estimated enrollment was 2,400,000.

Second, although 25 out of 2,400 colleges and universities in the United States received 39.5 percent of all foreign students in 1951–52 (see Appendix A), 1,354 institutions reported having one or more foreign students. Only 766 reported that none was enrolled. It seems fair to assume that a greater number of American institutions are now accepting foreign students than was the case in 1930. As a result more educators and more communities have become aware not only of the value of exchange of persons but also of "the foreign student problem."

Third, there has been both a relative and an absolute increase of students from countries whose cultures differ markedly from our own. Inspection of the data on distribution of foreign students by country of origin in 1930–31 and in 1951–52 (see Appendix B) indicates that the proportions of Latin-American, Near Eastern, and South Asian students have, by and large, increased more than the 300 percent over-all for these twenty years. The reason for these increases must be viewed in terms of short-range and long-range factors.

The short-range reasons for this increase are not hard to find. During the period of the Good Neighbor Policy in the late 1930's and early 1940's, the United States government encouraged Latin-American students to come to this country to study. The American public responded generously to government leadership. Moreover, during World War II many European universities were closed to students who would normally have gone to them; hence, they turned to institutions in the United States. World War II delayed the higher education of at least one and in some cases two or three academic generations in Europe and much of Asia. It isolated scholars, who, like the great international corporations, depend upon free intercourse across national boundaries for their vitality. American educational institutions passed relatively unscathed through the war whereas the human and material resources of universities in many parts of the world had been destroyed or severely damaged. After the war, the United States government launched massive democratization and re-education programs in Austria, Germany, Korea, and Japan that included study tours by nationals of those countries sent to the United States. Simultaneously, many of the technically underdeveloped nations launched programs of economic and social development that required trained personnel for whom educational facilities were not immediately available in the homelands. The pre-eminence of the United States in many technical and scientific fields made this country an obvious place to secure such training.

The justification for speaking of these as short-range factors is readily apparent. The wartime isolation of scholars, at least among free nations, is already disappearing. The wartime backlog of students has already diminished. The rehabilitation of European educational institutions and the development of new national or regional educational resources in other parts of the world are progressing. Although dollar shortages abroad promise to continue for some time, Congress does not seem likely to expand, and may not maintain, the appropriations voted for student exchange in the past.[3] The financial difficulties facing many American educational institutions suggest that they will not be inclined to take up any slack in public appropriations. Our own student population will be increasing rapidly for the next decade or two. The various large private foundations, although generous in their cross-cultural education grants, do not consider exchange of persons to be an end in itself. On

[3] In fiscal year 1952 the International Educational Exchange Service of the Department of State had a budget of $8.2 million. In fiscal year 1953 its dollar budget was $6.4 million. Counterpart funds are not included in this figure. (See U.S. Congress, Senate, *Overseas Information Programs of the United States: Report of the Committee on Foreign Relations*, 83rd Cong., 1st Sess., Senate, Report No. 406 (Washington: Government Printing Office, 1953), p. 79. These figures do not cover special appropriations for Germany, Austria, Finland, China, Korea, and in fiscal year 1953 India (under the India wheat bill). If much more than foreign student funds are included and counterpart funds are also added, the figures are $23.8 million for fiscal year 1952 and $23.3 million for fiscal year 1953.

the whole, their assistance to study abroad is highly selective and closely geared to other programmatic interests.[4]

The long-range factors that may affect the continued growth of the foreign student population in the United States are also varied and difficult to weigh. The ease of travel in the modern world and the attendant interest in areas formerly considered inaccessible are certainly not likely to diminish so long as political factors permit the pursuit of such interests. The world population is still increasing rapidly. The United States may well maintain its lead in technical and scientific studies. The importance of English as a world language has not only increased rapidly in the postwar period, but may well retain its position for many years to come with the result that a knowledge of English will be a greater drawing power in selecting a country for foreign study than it was a generation ago.

But in considering long-run factors, it must be recalled that as nations develop their own university systems, as English is more competently taught in these institutions, as technical and scientific know-how are acquired, some of the pull on foreign students that the United States now exerts may be reduced.

Thus, no firm conclusion can be reached about the net effect of all the long-run and short-run factors making for, or militating against, the continued growth of the foreign student population of the United States. We in America are prone to view our world in expanding rather than in stable or retrogressing terms. However, the foreign student population of this country may well be about stabilized or may even decrease. This by no means suggests that all who wish to study in the United States have come here. But unless academic requirements are lowered or academic entrance regulations are altered, unless massive drives for funds from private sources are made or dollar exchange eased, and unless our institutions expand sufficiently to accommodate our own increasing college and university popula-

[4] For example, see *Ford Foundation Annual Report for 1952*, p. 20.

tion, it seems unlikely that the foreign student population in the United States will continue to increase indefinitely. The task that lies ahead is that of qualitative improvement.

Here in the United States there is an important element in both the quantitative and qualitative situation that deserves at least passing mention. With the end of World War II the government and the people of the United States assumed a new position of responsibility in world affairs. The period of isolationism was at an end, and consequently any inclination to provincialism and uncritical self-satisfaction was sharply challenged. The tradition of citizen participation in national affairs was extended, *pari passu*, to international affairs. Also many Americans had brought back from wartime service abroad a quickened interest in particular countries. Individuals and private organizations sought avenues for assisting in the larger and more complex role of the nation. It became increasingly evident to many that these responsibilities extended beyond physical rebuilding after the destruction of war. Increasingly the issues were seen as long-range ones which were deeply rooted in intimate human experiences. Yet the problems were of such unaccustomed magnitude and complexity that men of good will were bewildered and discouraged in determining where best to direct their efforts.

Interest in the foreign students studying here, and a concern with broadening the opportunities for such study, seemed to offer a happy solution of this dilemma. It was an approach that promised to provide constructive and sympathetic action beneficial to the student and his country as well as to the participating Americans and their national interest.

This growth of interest after World War II is reminiscent of a similar development after World War I, when many of the older private international educational groups began or extended foreign study facilities. The German Academic Exchange Service, the Institute of International Education, the Belgian American Educational Foundation, Inc., the American-Scandinavian Foundation, and several of the American private foundations were only a few of the organizations that for various reasons placed great hope in international educational exchanges in that era. This tradition and many of the institutions associated with it still exist. They are faced with a readjustment and reappraisal of their goals and operational procedures not only in the light of present and future circumstances, but also in the light of our growing sophistication about the nature of individual and social processes.

The change in the mood and the goals of Americans interested in the field of study abroad is clearly demonstrated by comparing the literature appearing on the subject in 1954 with *The Foreign Student in America* which appeared in 1925.[5] The earlier volume was written with strongly religious overtones that are less evident today, but it nevertheless raised issues that are still debated. The study was undertaken in 1922 to define foreign students' needs and problems and to formulate an adequate program. The all-too-familiar questionnaire method was used and, then as now, the inadequacy of the method was deplored. It was recognized that some of the foreign students in the United States were potential leaders in their homelands. They were conceived of as ambassadors of good will and friendship between nations. In addition, a historical sketch of the shifts in the drawing powers of different countries, particularly of Germany and France, for students seeking international study opportunities throws salutary historical perspective on our present American role in that respect. The significance of different cultural backgrounds to adjustment in the United States was realized then as now. Attitudes toward the host country and their bearing on readjustment in the homeland were noted, although the phrasing was largely in terms of zeal to extend

[5] W. Reginald Wheeler, H. H. King, and A. B. Davidson (eds.), *The Foreign Student in America* (New York: Association Press, 1925).

mission efforts. The foreign students' criticisms of this country in 1925 have an entirely contemporary flavor. The Asian student then as now was a source of particular concern to analysts of student exchange.

Most of the practical suggestions made in 1925 have a familiar ring today,[6] and it is striking how many of these are well on their way to being implemented. Nevertheless, certain clear differences between the situation as reported in the 1925 survey and the present situation also emerge. These differences have both quantitative and qualitative aspects. In 1925 the organizations concerned with foreign students had not yet multiplied to the degree that they have today. Thirty years ago church people rather than educational administrators and public servants were prime movers in the field, although the personal needs and reactions of individual foreign students appear to remain much the same. Public funds formed no appreciable part of student support and, in general, financial aid was less generous than today. Self-support by foreign students was more nearly the rule. These shifts reflect social changes that have taken place, not only in this nation but also in others. Individual initiative and individual responsibility have diminished as central governments have developed in power, size, and complexity and as they have assumed steadily widening responsibilities for social services. The newer vocabulary of public administration and the applied social sciences is replacing the older language of the churches. The "managerial revolution" has intervened, and its influences are reflected in the administration of foreign student programs.

In sum, from 1930 to 1953 the foreign student population in the United States had increased 300 percent whereas during those same years our own student population had grown only 100 percent. Among foreign students, those coming from countries with markedly different cultural traditions are both abso-

[6] See Appendix C for some of these.

lutely and proportionately more numerous. These two factors as well as the marked development of interest in foreign relations have broadened and sensitized Americans to the whole field of student exchange. There is no way of predicting with assurance that the numbers of foreign students will increase in the future, but it does seem clear that qualitative improvements in dealing with our foreign guests is the next task before us. To this task both basic and applied social sciences have a contribution to make.

Chapter 2

VARIATIONS IN GOALS AND MOTIVES

THE PRECEDING chapter discussed causes and implications of quantitative changes during the past three decades in the foreign student population of the United States. Even a passing mention of the factors operating to produce such changes suggests the many types of goals and motives that are represented in student exchanges. In a free world quantitative increases are inevitably associated with diversification of interests. In other words, the more people who are involved in an activity, the greater is the likelihood that various goals and purposes will find expression as long as freedom is granted for their expression. With the many strands that now appear in the fabric of cross-cultural education, it is not astonishing that goals and motives should be varied and often conflicting. The field of foreign study is not only inherently complex, it is also beset by special pleading, inadequate knowledge, hidden motives, and the vague, or impractical, goals of both its proponents and antagonists.

In the present chapter, a number of the goals and motives of some of the participants in the foreign study field will be suggested.[1] The United States government, for example, is necessarily concerned that the students it sponsors acquire not only a deeper but also a more appreciative understanding of this country. This is a view most American citizens share. Although the enabling legislation of the Congress stresses education rather than propaganda as the instrument for achieving this goal, the intent is clear. Education is not equated with propaganda, but it is nevertheless envisaged as an instrument of foreign policy and of national interest.

On the other hand, the governments of nations intent upon economic and social development are not necessarily concerned that the fellowship students they send here acquire any very deep appreciation of American life. In fact, such appreciation may serve only to create in certain students disturbingly critical attitudes toward their own countries upon return. Rather, the intent of certain foreign governments in supporting exchange programs may extend no further than training in skills that will be relevant to the welfare of their nation. In some countries, students returning from America will be critically scrutinized to determine whether they have "sold out" to the United States. If they are too much "Americanized," they may find themselves handicapped.

To the educational world also a variety of purposes and expectations may be associated with foreign students. The administrator of a college may hope that the foreign students on the campus will help to liberalize and broaden the outlook

---

[1] An excellent statement of these goals was prepared by Mrs. Vandi Haygood of the Institute of International Education as part of the documentation for the May 17–18, 1954, meeting of the Committee on Educational Interchange Policy under the title, "Goals in Educational Interchange Programs: An Analysis of the Goals of Foreign Students and of United States Sponsoring Agencies" (Mimeographed). A more popular version of this study was issued by the Committee on Educational Interchange Policy under the title, *The Goals of Student Exchange: An Analysis of Goals of Programs for Foreign Students* (New York: The Institute, January 1955).

of the American students. He may be interested in assisting the Federal Government in carrying out its program of fostering American prestige abroad. Or, he may be looking only for expanded enrollment to maintain the college's solvency. Faculty members may on one level share some or all of the official goals; they may sympathize with the motives of various individuals, but their professional aspirations and institutional loyalties may set standards that run at cross-purpose to other goals and motives. The foreign student advisers, insofar as they assume roles that are different from those of the teacher or administrator, may in turn have special interests and their own professional expectations in relation to the foreign student field.

To many American citizens the goals of foreign student exchange may be no more clearly defined than "international understanding" with the associated hope for peace—a relationship, unfortunately, that history can neither prove nor disprove. The closeness of interpersonal contacts between Frenchmen and Germans for many centuries has not kept the peace between these two nations. The Japanese students who came to study in the United States after the Meiji restoration were not able to prevent the attack on Pearl Harbor. But it is equally possible to argue that without such interpersonal contacts across national boundaries, hostilities and separatism might have been even greater than they have been.

Furthermore, there is still a considerable portion of the American public that reacts to the foreign students as it does to other foreigners who have come as immigrants with the intention of transferring their loyalties to this country and of being assimilated. The assimilation of these immigrants has been one of the outstanding achievements of the nation. Although assimilation is directly opposed to the intent of most cross-cultural education programs, it still seems to operate more or less consciously in the approach of many citizens to foreign guests (see pages 166–67). Other Americans may be interested in foreign students as "specimens" of unusual cultures—a sort of tourism in reverse.

The foreign students themselves also bring with them a wide range of publicly avowed, privately admitted, and even unconscious motives and expectations. This range of personal purposes and motives is not easily determined. Anyone who has examined the application forms knows that the statements made on them are as conventional and stereotyped as are the expressed goals of various fellowship programs. Applicants learn very rapidly through a dozen different cues the reasons for study here that are expected of them and that should be publicly avowed. Formally expressed reasons usually mirror the expressed objectives of the sponsors of the programs. Parenthetically, these same ideas reappear all too frequently in the solicited statements that visitors make about the benefits derived from a study sojourn in this country. Courtesy and self-interest often dictate such replies.

The private objectives of foreign students are sometimes detectable in both the more forthright and the more naïve applicants. These may not necessarily reflect the intentions for which public or private monies may have been allocated. Some applicants express broad and unformulated curiosity about this country as a dominant world power and as leader of the democratic nations. They seem to feel that as one of the two great giants in this world, it is a spectacle well worth scrutinizing. Probably such students would have the same intellectual curiosity about the Union of Soviet Socialist Republics and would be as highly motivated to study in Russia for a year or two were it possible.

Some applicants have interwoven with curiosity about world powers a laudable sense of adventure and a desire to travel for its own sake. For those who accept a philosophy that equates experience and education, and for those Americans who themselves travel so eagerly and indefatigably, this alone should present an understandable and by no means unacceptable motive.

Some students are motivated by an eagerness to acquire new skills. They are task-centered individuals, representing one type of foreign guest. For many of these students, the acquisition of degrees may acquire what seems to many of their advisers and teachers a disproportionate importance. Some task-centered students may see the relevance of such skills to the welfare of their country; others may be little involved with idealistic notions of their nation's welfare. They may view study abroad as an opportunity for personal advancement and enhanced social capital on their return. We must not assume that such students are necessarily interested primarily in formal educational achievement. Their chief motive for a year's study in the United States may be to perfect their English, and not at all to acquire either skill or a master's degree in political science even though they may be registered in such courses. The fluent command of English plus American contacts may be far more important—and realistically important—for returning students than achievement in formal studies.

Still other students may be discouraged by their life chances in their homelands, and a fellowship opportunity may appear to them as the first step toward possible emigration. For example, an Austrian student may have lost his family during the war; he may have found economic and professional opportunities limited at home; he may view darkly the political future of his homeland; he may estimate that if he can once reach the United States, his opportunities for upward economic and social mobility will be enhanced. (Many Americans are familiar with this situation in reverse. Young Americans who see no opportunity of being admitted to our medical schools have crowded into more accessible European medical centers rather than abandon their ambitions.) It seems to be true that many unmarried women students from widely diverse countries hope that marriage to an American citizen may result from a study sojourn here.

Some of these private objectives may not appear as legitimate to certain officials or educators, but this kind of so-called "escapism" is fully understandable in human and individual terms. One cannot but admire the hopefulness, the energy, and the initiative that motivate such persons. These were among the motives that brought our immigrant population to this country. It is also necessary to realize that motives may be personally important but socially irrelevant. Short of complete thought control by the state, every human being probably faces at one time or another the essential problem of relating his private motives to social imperatives.

Obviously, each individual's desire to study in the United States may be assumed to be a complex bundle of formal but honestly held reasons, of privately held objectives, and of unconscious needs. No single and simple factor is operative in the heterogeneous impulses that move men and women to study beyond the boundaries of their homelands. There is perhaps some virtue in recognizing that many legitimate reasons, objectives, and motives are operative both within a single individual and among different individuals. The planners and administrators of any fellowship program may legitimately set a particular, even a rigid, goal for the expenditure of their funds, particularly if they are public funds. It would then be wise not to have the same goals set for all programs, but to encourage many and diverse sources of funds and to encourage many and diverse objectives that meet not only our own varied motives and expectations but also those of our guests.

Conformity presents a very real problem to us in America. Fortunately, this is being more widely recognized. We are given to fads and fashions of opinion, we are inclined to climb on band wagons, we like clear-cut issues and efficient formulae and definite solutions. When we think we have found them, we are inclined to consider them self-evident and compelling and to expect everyone to fall into line with them. All this often leads us to strive for the efficiencies of regulations and centralization. We may in the process lose the qualities of heterogeneity and forget that a "tolerance for ambiguity" is the essence of a functioning democracy.

Perhaps one generalization emerges. The goals and the motives of foreign study must be educational. But we must understand education in its broadest sense—as both formal and informal learning experiences. Whenever the foreign student, or his American sponsor, injects goals or motives that are inappropriate or irrelevant to education, broadly conceived, or uses education as an instrument to other ends, there is the risk that the good and ancient tradition of study abroad will be damaged. If we cling to education as a worthy goal in itself, we, and our foreign guests, are less likely to experience disappointments and frustrations and less likely to react petulantly. We need to remember that learning is in itself a worthy goal even though it does not necessarily assure world peace, economic development, or a generic enthusiasm for the United States. Should cross-cultural education actually contribute to world peace, economic development of the home country, and a positive appreciation of the host country, these must be considered fortunate and perhaps almost fortuitous adjuncts. Neither we nor our foreign guests must expect to saw down a tree with a nail file. The expectations and motives of all partners in this enterprise must be appropriate to the instrument employed. If we are providing educational opportunities, we and our guests must expect education to be the primary goal.

Chapter 3

ROLE OF THE FEDERAL GOVERNMENT IN THE FOREIGN STUDENT FIELD

A LARGE environment presumably influences the small environments of which it is constituted. "Before the idea of influence we ought to be far more puzzled than we are; if we find it hard to be puzzled enough, we may contrive to induce the proper state of uncertainty. . . ."[1] All student exchange, and even more significantly, federally subsidized or controlled programs for exchange, will be influenced by foreign policy and the climate of international relations. But it is important to avoid a simple one-to-one assumption of relationship between foreign policies and international relations on one hand and its small environment, student exchange, on the other hand. A negative or mistaken policy toward another nation may have a negative influence on the foreign study sojourn of their nationals. For example, when the United States Congress debated attaching political conditions to the shipments of wheat

[1] Lionel Trilling, "The Sense of the Past," *The Liberal Imagination* (New York: Doubleday, 1953), p. 188.

18

needed in the famine areas of India, the interpersonal relations between Americans and Indians both in that country and in this country worsened. On the other hand, Indians and Americans who develop a warm concern for each other and some knowledge of each other's national values will never again so easily allow fluctuations of foreign policy to form the sole basis of their relationships and judgments concerning each other.

Contact and study abroad are small environments within the larger environment of foreign policy and international relations. They cannot determine either foreign policy or international relations, but are undoubtedly elements in the larger situation. Whether a central government should concern itself with all the elements that constitute its international relations or should confine itself to the traditional role of formulating foreign policy is a question of the values individuals hold and of their philosophy of the state.

People in this country differ in their views on the role the Federal Government should play in the affairs of the nation and its citizens. There are those who believe that the Federal Government should provide leadership; that it must, therefore, be large; that it should be staffed by imaginative people who are given opportunities for creative work. Others believe that the Federal Government should follow rather than lead the electorate; that it should be as small as is consistent with our national interest; that it should be staffed with public servants prepared to serve conscientiously any administrative policy given to them. The same practical issue can be stated with somewhat different implications if we see the issue as one between people who think of government as a service state and those who see it only as a mechanism for the protection and resolution of differences.[2] These two views of the role of the Federal Government have never been fully nor permanently resolved in our

[2] The writer is indebted to Cyril O. Houle for this second way of phrasing the question.

national history, and the individual's philosophic inclinations on the matter may bias, more or less consciously, his reactions to the role of the Federal Government in the foreign student field.

In addition, there is a great deal of confusion about the various agencies and their functions in relation to educational exchange programs. This confusion is understandable. From 1946 to 1953, thirteen laws were passed by Congress for educational exchange programs of one sort or another.

Congress appropriates money for these purposes to seven different agencies which in turn allocate funds to 30 other federal agencies. . . . The job-pyramiding resulting from the contracting and subcontracting arrangements by these many agencies, it has been reported in extreme cases, results in the use of 30 percent of the appropriated funds for administrative purposes.[3]

This description, however, is applicable primarily to the variety of leader, trainee, and various visitor programs rather than to the role played by the International Educational Exchange Service (IES) of the Department of State in its handling of foreign students. The International Educational Exchange Service has on the whole properly eschewed any very large role in direct operations, and its inbound student contracts are largely centralized in one private contracting agency with over thirty years of experience in the field, namely, the Institute of International Education. In 1953, when 193 educators and 77 business and organization executives were queried by the United States Advisory Commission on Educational Exchange, no academic institution suggested de-emphasizing the role of government, whereas 14 percent (11) of business and other organizations did so suggest. However, 22 percent (42) of the academic institutions and 34 percent (26) of the business and organiza-

---

[3] U.S. Congress, Senate, *Overseas Information Programs of the United States: Hearings before a Subcommittee of the Committee on Foreign Relations,* 82nd Cong., 2nd Sess., Nov. 20–21, 1952 (Washington: Government Printing Office, 1953), pp. 163–64.

tional groups stated they thought too many agencies were involved.[4] It would appear that the respondents were in many instances unsure of the category of educational exchanges which they had in mind and that legitimate criticisms of some programs were extended unjustifiably to the inbound foreign students handled by the International Educational Exchange Service.[5]

Both officials and teaching personnel urgently need fuller knowledge about varying programs and regulations, although governmental and private agencies have made continuing efforts along this line. Too often our foreign guests bear the brunt of inadequate information, and at the same time legislators and administrators are deprived of the kind of appropriate guidance that citizen groups should provide.

In what follows, reference is largely limited to the International Educational Exchange Service's inbound foreign student program as it operated from the years 1952 to 1954 and to a set of fundamental notions about it. The first point that needs to be considered is the size of the program in relation to the total foreign student population in the United States. In 1952 government funds of $2,067,373 were allocated for 1,777 foreign students. To meet additional needs of these same students, private funds amounting to $667,073 were obtained through the Institute of International Education, and still other private funds for them from other sources amounted to $1,352,654. In other words, the government allocation of over $2 million for 1,777 foreign students was approximately evenly matched by private contributions in order to support this number of students. In congres-

---

[4] Bureau of Social Science Research, American University, *The Student Exchange Program: An Appraisal by 193 Educators and 77 Business and Organization Executives*, prepared for the International Evaluation Staff, IIA, Dept. of State (Dittoed; Washington, January 1953), pp. 30 and 34.

[5] A review of U.S. government exchange programs is contained in Helen A. Miller's article, "U.S. Government Programs of International Exchange: 1952," *The Educational Record*, October 1953, pp. 313–26. The Department of State's foreign leader (as opposed to student) program is described by James A. Donavan in the same issue of *The Educational Record*.

sional hearings this was taken as evidence of popular support for the government program.[6]

The following points emerge when these sums of money and numbers of students are related to the total foreign student population in the United States. The IES budgets $2,800 per student per year including six weeks' orientation but excluding international travel. This obviously does not cover the overhead and salaries of State Department officers, of the Institute of International Education, of faculties and universities, or hospitality by American citizens, and the expenses privately met by a student. Probably $5,000 per person for one year of study including transportation to and from a reasonably distant country more nearly represents the true per-capita expenditure involved for a year's study in the United States. Disregarding the source of funds, making a rough deduction for the international travel of students who stay two or more years, and multiplying by 32,000 students, it seems likely that $130 million are spent annually for and by foreign students in the United States.

But since such estimates are necessarily hazardous, one can accept the unrealistically conservative figure of $3,000 per year per capita. When multiplied by 32,000 students, the total outlay would be reduced to $96 million annually. Even at this rate the IES student allocation of $2 million represents less than 2 percent of the total financial outlay for and by foreign students in the United States.

The policy of using federal funds to supplement partial awards from private sources has helped to stretch federal grants among a larger number of grantees. For example, Fulbright travel money can be used to pay the transportation of students who furnish the rest of their own support or who receive support from private United States sources. Since any student who receives any government monies is considered to be affiliated with the International Educational Exchange Service, IES-

[6] These figures are drawn from *Overseas Information Programs of the United States, op. cit.,* p. 189.

affiliated students constitute 10-12 percent of all foreign students in the United States despite the fact that the funds allocated are equivalent to full coverage for only 1 percent to 2 percent of the foreign student population. Thus, the affiliational outreach of the IES is considerably greater than its financial outlay. It is, therefore, somewhat astonishing that the State Department's activities seem to loom so large in the minds of many people, even those who are well acquainted with the total field.

The importance attached to the State Department's activities indicates that the influence exerted by IES in the field has been greater than its financial outlay and that it has exercised a leadership role. Many divergent and often contradictory views have been expressed on this leadership role.

It is often said that government leadership in the field of educational exchanges runs the risk of being interpreted abroad as subverting education to propaganda. Certainly, government officials and their various advisory groups have not been insensitive to this risk. A step to correct such impressions was taken in 1953 when the educational exchange programs were left in the Department of State instead of being transferred out of the Department with the informational services of the United States. Even though this was a sound step, it does not fully meet the criticisms from abroad, and still falls short of divorcing foreign educational aid programs from governmental jurisdiction. The quasi-official British Council, for example, established with its own board of directors and operating on a five-year grant, goes further in that direction than any solution so far suggested in the United States.[7]

[7] For a comparative but somewhat dated study of cultural relations programs of ten countries including the United States and the United Kingdom in which the development of the British Council is discussed, see Ruth E. McMurry and Muna Lee, *The Cultural Approach: Another Way in International Relations* (Chapel Hill: University of North Carolina Press, 1947). Another excellent statement of the development of cultural relations by the U.S. government is contained in Ben M. Cherrington's "Ten Years After: Ten Years of Intercultural Relations," *Association of American Colleges Bulletin*, December 1948, pp. 500–522.

A second comment made on government programs is that any administrative agency, under pressure from Congress for annual appropriations, is forced to stress national interest rather than education. This view has cogency only to the extent that national interests and educational goals are assumed to be mutually incompatible. Such incompatability need not be inherent. Conflicts in this realm are more likely to rest upon administrative regulations than on broadly stated goals as such. Thus, the postwar German and Japanese democratization and re-education programs seemed often to work at cross-purposes with the best interests of genuine education in matters of selection, duration of the sojourn, the numbers, and geographic distribution of visitors in the United States—all essentially matters in the realm of administrative regulations devised to implement the programs and not inherently conflicting with educational goals.

A third view of government exchange programs is that they tend to be inflexible on two scores—that administrative regulations tend to be overgeneralized, and policies cannot be altered rapidly enough to meet changing situations. This view would have greatest validity were it applicable to enabling legislation, since such legislation binds the executive and does not lend itself to rapid change. In fact, much of the enabling legislation is so broadly worded that there is latitude within its framework for executive units to set operational policy. Such regulations and policies can be altered so long as citizens' advisory groups diligently perform the functions assigned to them and so long as the government staff is genuinely cooperative. For example, until recently Fulbright travel grants were valid for one year only, and, although exceptions could be made, the process was administratively cumbersome. It was urged that the policy was operating to the disadvantage of the grantees and the intent of the program. In the course of the next two or three years, this regulation was altered, and Fulbright travel grants have now been extended to a maximum of three years.

A fourth view of government exchange programs—that they are vacillating and have short-range objectives—seems in one sense to contradict the third view stated above. It is said that vacillation and short-range objectives can be attributed to the system of annual appropriations and to shifts in national interest that do not necessarily coincide with long-range educational purposes. The generous support of Latin-American educational exchange before and during World War II and its subsequent drastic curtailment is cited as a case in point. Some educators and many national planners believe that intercultural exchanges, to be effective, must be based on long-term planning and that they should not be subjected to fluctuations of short-range political considerations.

A fifth viewpoint is that government agencies are inclined to build up administrative staffs that duplicate the administrative and operational staffs of their contracting agencies, whether private or public, and certainly dual control and review are both cumbersome and costly. This opinion is extremely difficult to appraise objectively. It is not possible from published statements to arrive at an accurate estimate of the size and functions of staffs employed in foreign student programs in government, in private contracting agencies, and in educational institutions that are concerned solely with the contributions made from public monies. One encounters in this area the same difficulties of categorization and the same imponderables that prevent a reliable estimate of the true per-capita cost of foreign students in the United States. Both of these questions deserve objective investigation.

A sixth view of the role of government agencies in the foreign student field is that—quite apart from duplication—they complicate administrative procedures, and thus increase overhead costs both in government and private agencies. Again, no firm substantiation of this view can be extracted from published sources. However, it does seem probable that the accountability by government servants for the disposition of public funds in the public interest does require types and numbers of procedures that do not necessarily encumber purely private operations. Certainly the relatively simple procedure for study abroad which obtained at the beginning of the century has been greatly bureaucratized, especially and perhaps inevitably when government grants are involved. The application form alone, which represents the first contact of a candidate with the American scene, ran to fifteen pages in 1954. However, most aspects of life today carry a heavy burden of administrative and managerial overhead, and it is not only government bureaucracies the world over that are given to paper work. Whether the actual fiscal contribution and the attendant services of the government —for example, overseas selection committees—offset this apparently inescapable condition of government participation cannot at this stage be definitely answered. There can be no denial that as our foreign student program now functions the administrative complexity is formidable.

A seventh view often advanced is that the size and relative compactness of the government's foreign student program facilitates experiments in procedures and practices that would not be possible in diffuse and scattered private efforts. In this connection, the government sponsorship of, and experiments in, orientation procedures are often cited. Another instance is its growing emphasis on full awards. Still another case in point is its evaluation of programs.

An eighth view is that the magnitude of government monies for foreign students tends to deflect funds that might be contributed from private sources, a view that is difficult to prove or disprove. It is noteworthy that in 1952 the $2 million of government funds were matched from private sources. From the congressional viewpoint this is evidence of the leadership and also the popularity of the government's efforts. Certainly the foreign currencies made available through the Fulbright Act (Public Law 584) could not have been provided in so constructive a context from private sources.

In summary, it appears that government as the single largest contributor plays a role disproportionate to its actual fiscal contribution. Whether that influence is desirable or undesirable cannot in some instances be unequivocably demonstrated. In other instances, whether the influence exercised is desirable or undesirable is a function of the flexibility of its operational policies and of the degree of administrative restraint employed. In both these areas private organizations—whether educational institutions, administrating agencies, professional associations, or advisory committees—must assume considerable responsibility for the guidance of public servants and the establishment of constructive policies. The many groups that have been consulted or established by the government itself for this purpose indicate the desire on the part of the International Education Exchange Service to be responsive to such guidance.

Throughout the world ease of movement is being promoted by modern methods of transportation while freedom of movement is being restricted by the growing power of states over the lives of nationals. But if we in the United States are sincerely convinced of the desirability of free exchange of peoples and ideas, we should smooth the way for "the wandering scholar who has never shown much skill in finding his way through a tangle of regulations." [8]

[8] "The Wandering Scholar," *The Economist*, Dec. 19, 1953.

Chapter 4

COMPARATIVE PERSPECTIVE

The sense of concern about foreign students in the United States during the postwar period has been attributed to a number of interacting factors. More citizens and schools are seeing more foreign students and are also meeting students from previously unfamiliar cultures. The desire of individuals and groups to participate more fully in the new international responsibilities of the United States has served to increase and intensify contacts with these students. The inevitable disparity in the goals of programs and the motives of individuals has sometimes led to misunderstandings. A steadily widening managerial emphasis in modern life, including the role of government, has enlarged and also complicated the situation. These may not represent all the factors that are operative, but even these few serve to account for the "problem of the foreign student" and the concern it has engendered in many quarters.

It is often helpful to view one's own problems from a broader perspective and to realize that other nations also deal in their own fashion with comparable situations. By 1947, twenty-nine nations had adopted intercultural exchanges, in one form or another, as an instrument of national policy.[1] The governments of Europe have enlarged prewar appropriations or created new ones to encourage foreign students to enroll in their educational institutions. The governments of many technically under-developed countries appreciated the need for financing study abroad by personnel they were not yet prepared to train at home; for example, "Chinese Communists in 1953 are reportedly enrolling in their schools some 5,000 students from Indonesia, Malaya, Borneo, Hong Kong and Macao."[2]

International agencies have also sponsored programs of educational exchange for both technical and idealistic reasons. In 1948, the first year that UNESCO published *Study Abroad*, it listed 672 fellowship programs offering 15,070 study opportunities. In 1952, only four years later, the number of programs had increased to 1,893 and the study opportunities to 43,000.[3] While a part of this increase may be accounted for by better data-collecting, it also represents a real increase in programs, both governmental and private.

It must be recognized, however, that awards cannot be equated with students since one student may need more than one type of award to finance his study. The 1,747 institutions providing UNESCO either directly or indirectly with information reported a total of 85,162 foreign students in 1951–52.[4] It would probably be no exaggeration to put the total number of foreign students outside the iron curtain countries at 100,000. The numbers who are supported by personal funds must approximate 60,000.

Of the 85,162 foreign students reported in 1952, 32,359 were

[1] National Association of Foreign Student Advisers, *Handbook for Counselors of Students from Abroad* (Experimental ed.; 1949; New York: The Association, n.d.), p. 13.

[2] *New York Times* report from Canton, Aug. 13, 1953.

[3] United Nations Educational, Scientific and Cultural Organization, *Study Abroad: International Handbook of Fellowships, Scholarships, Educational Exchange 1952–53* (Paris: UNESCO, 1953), V, 5.

[4] *Ibid.*, p. 22.

studying in 18 European countries. This means that Europe, with a much smaller number of educational institutions, was carrying about the same foreign student load as the United States. The traditional prestige of many European universities, the comparatively lower cost of travel and living, and the scarcity of dollars, serve to offset the overwhelmingly larger number of awards made available by the United States.

The United Kingdom in 1952 was host to 7,622 students, of whom 4,189 were from the British Commonwealth overseas. The largest single national group was the Indian with a total of 831. The University of London alone enrolled 3,152 foreign students in that year, although the foreign student population in the United Kingdom was scattered among 23 institutions.[5] Switzerland in 1952 had a foreign student population of 4,004 compared to her own student population of 11,493. In other words, about 25 percent of all students in nine Swiss educational institutions were from abroad. At the University of Geneva, which is avowedly a particular case, almost 50 percent of its student body was foreign.[6] The University of Paris in 1952 enrolled 2,140 colonial students and 5,760 foreign students, compared to a French student body of 51,709;[7] about 17 percent of the student population was from outside France. This compares to the maximum number of foreign students that the Massachusetts Institute of Technology will admit. Foreign students comprise about 7 percent of the enrollment at the University of Amsterdam, a number considered "not impressive" by a professor of political science in that institution.[8] Even

[5] *Yearbook of the Universities of the Commonwealth: 1953* (London: G. Bell & Sons, 1953), p. 1571.

[6] *Schweizerischer Hochschul-Kalender (Almanach Universitaire Suisse)* 87. Ausgabe, 1952–53 (Zurich: Verlag Leemann, 1953), p. 117.

[7] *Université de Paris: Livret de l'Etudiant: 1952–53* (Paris: Presses Universitaires de France, 1953), p. 42.

[8] Jan Barents, "The University of Amsterdam and World Affairs," in Carnegie Endowment for International Peace, *Universities and World Affairs,* Document 22 (Mimeographed; New York: The Endowment, 1953), p. 6.

these scattered figures indicate that the colleges and universities of the United States as a whole, and even its institutions that have the heaviest foreign student enrollment, are not carrying an unusual or disproportionate share of the world population of students abroad.

The differences among the various countries in the machinery for handling and the attitudes toward this enrollment present a challenging question. The absence of any extensive data on the subject from Europe may be an indication that the question is viewed less seriously there than here. Certainly, there is no corps of administrators and counselors for foreign students comparable to that in this country. Similarly, the supportive machinery seems less complex and is probably less costly. A few scattered conversations with concerned individuals in England, France, and Switzerland suggest a far more relaxed attitude toward foreign students than in the United States. Probably many factors are operative to explain this position, among them a tolerance for cosmopolitan groups that is associated with little desire to assimilate, or favorably impress, foreigners. In Japan also, where there are considerable numbers of foreign students, no elaborate organization and sense of concern are observable.

In the United States, our highly developed system of counseling and administration in educational institutions is inevitably extended to foreign students. Not to do so would be discriminatory and would falsify the picture of our educational characteristics. The concern we extend to our own student body has been described by those unaccustomed to it as "spoon-feeding." If we appear to "spoon-feed" and to be overly concerned about foreign students, it is simply that we are acting in a fashion consistent with our own patterned behavior.

The views of at least one person of considerable experience with foreign students both here and abroad portray the American situation with a sharp lightness born of comparative perspective.

This sense of concern is related to, or partially manifested by, our undoubted compulsion to lead and guide foreign students from portal to portal, with compassionate shudders for their cultural shock, with a vast desire for them to behave like normal sophomores from South Bend, and with scientific sympathy for their neuroses. . . . Other countries are also hosts to large numbers of foreign students, some of them perhaps in proportion equal to the United States. While evidence is fragmentary, it may well be that other countries do not suffer from (enjoy?) this American sense of concern to nearly such a marked degree.

Have we created the "problem of the foreign student" more or less on purpose, in our own image? Have we, by adopting the running presumption that the foreign student *must* be a quivering mass of problems, encouraged a jungle-growth of a great, loose-jointed apparatus in this country which makes problems inevitable? Are we, as a country, by nurturing the proliferation of mechanisms which express our "concern" pricing ourselves out of the foreign student market? Have we, by means of refining and perfecting our machinery for tinkering with foreign students, placed strains upon those students to which only the magnificently resilient are impervious, and from which the principal beneficiaries are the hopelessly non-self-sufficient among the foreign student population?

I certainly do not pretend to know the answers to these questions, but for two years I was employed for the sole purpose of being "concerned"—in my case, to "evaluate"—the Army's Japanese exchange program. I know that from the moment a Japanese student inquired about the exchange opportunity, a whole host of "concerned" persons began, in succession, to go to work on him. The pattern is familiar: application forms, examinations, interviews, indoctrination receptions by the foreign office, placement interviews, shipboard orientation, and stateside orientation—the latter complete with guidance, counseling, random iterations of goals and objectives, visitations from agency personnel, questionnaires—and throughout the whole an atmosphere from which it is obvious to the most insensitive clod among the students that the Americans are on pins and needles to see if he is becoming properly "adjusted." And then, the man is ready to go to school, where the foreign student adviser, his IIE supervisor, and the good folk of the community can get a crack at him.

I am not belittling (or even trying to consider here) the benefits that accrue from all this. Anyhow, there is a sort of massive inevitability about it in this country. I do know, however, that for many (and many) a Japanese student the sheer weight of all these manifestations of concern have created a vast, vague, and sometimes overwhelming sense of obligation. They have been hedged about on all sides by people and groups which seem to be making an inscrutably and esoterically complex exercise out of the essentially simple matter of coming to the United States to go to school. Many of the Japanese students I know felt themselves placed in the really intolerable position of thinking they had to consider every action, every judgment, all their outward behavior, and often the inner condition of their souls in the light of whether these accorded with their hugely-felt but non-understood obligations. I could not count the number of times I have been asked: "But what do you expect of us?"

With reluctance a final note of sobriety must be injected. We must remind ourselves that there are in the United States still great numbers of students from abroad who do not encounter the "foreign student industry" (as one person designated it), and who quite competently manage their affairs without needing or arousing "concern." In later chapters an attempt is made to suggest a happy medium between oversolicitude and no solicitude within the wider pattern of American educational practice with respect to "guidance."

PART TWO

The Foreign Student

THE FOREIGN student" is perhaps a legitimate term for an immigration officer to use since it does describe a legal and administrative category of persons. But for purposes of study, to treat a great variety of foreign students as a single category is a human and scientific monstrosity. Actually, those who come to this country to pursue their education are of an infinite variety of nationalities, temperaments, and backgrounds. If one is concerned with the processes and factors affecting them, it seems wise to begin with individuals. To object to the term, *the* foreign student, may seem to be a matter of semantics, but there is a risk of intellectual confusion in simple matters of language. Once a collective term like *the* foreign student has been carelessly accepted, there is the attendant risk of careless verbs and qualifiers. One drops too easily into phrases such as *"the* foreign student adviser" instead of considering the many kinds of advisers that foreign students may need or at least encounter. Then *"the* foreign student" must be shown hospitality, or *"the* foreign student" has a language handicap. Foreign students constitute so heterogeneous a population that generalizations about them are suspect.

Granting, therefore, that we must deal with many foreign students and with individuals as our referents, the problem becomes one of trying to find valid orders of generalization in this complex field. It is certainly not the kind of field that opens easily to strict or rigorous scientific inquiry, but is an area given by practical considerations. The pure researcher who undertakes studies on foreign students finds himself forced to draw upon the full stock of concepts and methods he has at his command. The very nature of the area of inquiry suggests that cross-disciplinary research will be entailed if adequate formulations are to be evolved.[1]

In what follows an attempt is made to isolate salient factors that seem operative in foreign students' predeparture outlooks, their adaptations to American life, and their readjustments to the homeland. We shall, therefore, be concerned with certain generalizations and conjectures concerning the adaptive processes of individuals who move across boundaries not only of national states but also of languages and cultures.

At this stage value judgments are not to be attached to words like "adjustment" or "adaptation." Nor is "assimilation" implied. Rather, primary concern centers on the psychological adequacy of foreign students in dealing with unfamiliar situations. Concern for what happens, rather than its "goodness" or "badness," must constitute the initial approach in objective inquiries. If one is concerned with understanding these processes, then definitions of such terms as "adjustment," "adaptation," and "readjustment" will be end-products and not a point of departure in any investigation of the human aspects of cross-cultural education. It is nevertheless useful to employ such imprecise words as prerequisites to further thinking in the area.

Lastly, a brief comment on method: In the American scene,

---

[1] The material in this portion of the book derives almost wholly from the joint thinking of participants in the first phase of research carried out under the auspices of the Social Science Research Council's Committee on Cross-Cultural Education in 1952–53. General statements on the subject and the names of the participants are to be found in Social Science Research Council, *Items,* Vol. 6, No. 1, and Vol. 7, No. 3.

considerable confidence is placed on quantitative statements derived from questionnaires or comparable instruments. No such rigor of method underlies most of what follows here. To the writer, quantification and the associated use of instruments appear appropriate only after some conceptual clarity has been introduced into a field, after some sense exists of the kind and relative significance of the variables that are operative. So far quantitative studies have been used largely to evaluate operations. For example, questionnaires have sought information on student reactions to orientation courses. While these are useful exercises, they do not measurably advance an understanding of the processes involved. A great deal of methodologically rigorous research may be expended on relatively trivial or obvious questions and issues unless it is pursued within the framework of broad and explicit conceptual formulations.

Chapter 5

SALIENT FACTORS IN
PREARRIVAL ATTITUDES

IF ONE recognizes that a study period in the United States is only a fragment of the total life experience of an individual, and if one attempts to understand this total experience as an on-going process, then a study sojourn abroad is seen in its proper episodic perspective. But for each student the episode will have varying significance: He brings to his journey idiosyncratic qualities and the distillation of his own life experiences, and he brings to it also familial, social, and national conditionings ranging from those gained in educational institutions in his homeland to national values which he shares in some degree with his countrymen. He arrives in a new country with certain emotional needs, certain cognitive sets, and certain more or less realistic expectations.

It is not easy to generalize the factors that are significantly operative in these prearrival sets, but preliminary investigations suggest certain salient constellations. Some of these are not usually explicit in the minds of the newly arrived student. Some are heavily overlaid and distorted; these are the currently fashionable stereotypes. Similarly, many of these factors are still inadequately formulated or are even ignored by persons here in the United States who have responsibilities for these guests.

It may, therefore, be useful to review briefly some of these factors.

In the succeeding pages the following themes will be raised: the crucial importance of self-esteem, the relation of self-esteem to felt and accorded national status as modified by the individual's degree of involvement in his nation's status, the functions of racial and other discriminations as they bear on self-esteem, the consequences of the student's role as a cultural ambassador, firmness of anchorage in the homeland and its relation to life expectancies and life chances, the extent of prior cross-cultural experience, and the political relations between the home and the host country. All these factors and many others serve to create the image of the United States that each student brings with him to this country. The specific content of these images is not discussed here, in part because the subject has been treated elsewhere [1] and in part because such images appear to be highly changeable.

Self-Esteem

First, it is assumed, on the basis of considerable evidence, that the positive and constructive adjustment of a foreign guest to any new society, nation, or culture, requires that he have a healthy self-esteem. It is also assumed that a foreign sojourn should not diminish it. Rather, foreign study should enhance an individual's self-esteem, deepen it, and broaden it. This is a value judgment with which, presumably, few will quarrel.

We then immediately are faced with what constitutes a "healthy" self-esteem. How does one diagnose whether self-esteem is being diminished or enhanced? Actually, the symptoms of diminished self-esteem are not too difficult to detect. We are all familiar with defense mechanisms employed by

[1] Richard D. Lambert (ed.), "America through Foreign Eyes," *The Annals of the American Academy of Political and Social Science,* Vol. 295 (1954).

normal as well as by disturbed personalities when they feel themselves on unsure ground. Foreign students are no exception. If their self-esteem is insufficiently resilient, they may react with depression and withdrawal. Or, they may indulge in compensatory strivings and often an inappropriate redoubling of effort that in extreme cases may even resemble obsessional perseverance. These are the students who work themselves to death. Or, they may react with openly expressed hostility that involves the rejection of the host nation and a compensatory chauvinism. Another type of defensive reaction may be over-identification, as when students become more American than the Americans.

These mechanisms are frequently and normally employed by persons facing threats to their self-esteem. These are the reactions that need to be quickly recognized when they arise. But more important, in these days of "preventive medicine" and "mental health," such reactions should be dealt with by wise counseling and by adjusting environmental factors.

On the other hand, manifestations of a healthy self-esteem are easily recognized. Enhanced self-esteem in a foreign guest may be manifest in a positive feeling toward the host country without surrendering the ability to appraise its strengths and weaknesses objectively. An enhanced self-esteem may also be manifest in a realistic expansion of the student's goals and aspirations both in terms of his sojourn abroad and in terms of his life ambitions at home. Fortunately, there is some evidence that a considerable proportion of the foreign students in the United States do experience just this kind of healthy development.

Many factors affect self-esteem. For example, one set of factors lies in the field of institutional education. The student's opportunities to study what he wants, where he wants, with whom he wants, can bulk large in enhancing his self-esteem. Similarly, his own linguistic, intellectual, and temperamental capabilities may be crucial in fulfilling his educational aspirations. Educational opportunities and capabilities may in fact be a more important factor than national status. These various educational factors have been stressed repeatedly and are not likely to be overlooked.

Another set of factors that may have marked influence on an individual's self-esteem in cross-cultural adaptation is his capacity to establish early in his sojourn one or more supportive interpersonal relationships. Such relationships may be friendships—male or female—with Americans or fellow-nationals or fellow-foreign students. They may also be found in the relationship of a teacher to the student, or the finding of a parent or sibling substitute. They may even be found in a sponsor or protégé relationship. This subject will be raised later in several contexts.

Lastly there appears to be a relationship between self-esteem and national status. However, these must not be interpreted as having a simple one-to-one casual relationship.

National Status and Self-Esteem

Many individuals appear to establish, more or less consciously, national status hierarchies. Some people may conceive of national status as a continuum. For example, nations may be ranged from the least technically developed to the most highly technically developed. Here the elements usually chosen for establishing a scale are such indices as per capita income, gross national product, the number of automobiles, or infant mortality. This is a form of evaluation of national status much in vogue in the United States. Other people see national status as a series of typologies. For example, countries may be grouped as the "materialistic" nations of the West and the "spiritual" nations of the East, or as the colonial or imperial nations. Others recognize religious typologies like Islamic, Christian, Buddhist.

In general, most ideas about national status seem to be based on a highly selected series of traits, and most people's ideas about national status appear to be highly value-laden.

However important an objective study of national status may be in the long run, and however fascinating this type of speculation has proved for philosophic historians, littérateurs, and social scientists, the immediate, practical, and relevant point is the view any particular foreign student holds in this respect. What the student conceives as the status of his nation, particularly in comparison to the host country, is usefully designated as *felt national status*. Reciprocally, what individuals in the host country conceive to be the status of the student's country is usefully designated as *accorded national status*. If the foreign student's felt national status ranks considerably higher than the status accorded his country in the host nation, then the adjustment he makes may diminish his self-esteem.

It may be worth underlining that direct hostility on the part of the host to a particular nationality is not necessarily the most damaging attitude to a foreigner's self-esteem. Pure ignorance and naïve stereotypes may be even more demeaning to a foreign student's self-esteem. A Thai will not feel that his country has been accorded high national status if the only image of his country his American friends possess is based on the charming musical comedy *The King and I*. Dr. Lambert in his study of Indian students at the University of Pennsylvania [2] indicates that affronts to Indian national sensitivity are almost unavoidable in the United States where our primary interest in India seems to center on caste, child marriages, famine, disease, and Hindu-Moslem tensions. Indian students rarely escape repeated cross-examination on these subjects during an American sojourn any

[2] Richard D. Lambert and Marvin Bressler, "Preliminary Report: Indian Students Project at the University of Pennsylvania," submitted to Committee on Cross-Cultural Education of the Social Science Research Council, October 1953 (Mimeographed).

more than Americans abroad escape cross-questioning on our race relations, nationalism, and atomic power. Nor is the student of either country likely to overcome quickly his defensive reactions.

The next element in the nexus we are here considering is not so much the perceived national status as the degree to which an individual's self-esteem is involved in the status of his country. There are people whose image of the self is deeply invested in being American, French, or Indian nationals, but there are also other people whose self-concept is remarkably free of such symbolic identifications. An American studying in France may value himself more highly, for example, because he is the citizen of a country generally conceded to be among the most powerful in the world. A Danish student may value himself as a scientist and not because Denmark is considered an admirable country. A deeply patriotic Nigerian may feel that his country is still young and technically underdeveloped, and his sensitivities and insecurities may be heightened when studying in Sweden.

It is a preliminary notion that students from colonial areas or from newly independent countries are more likely—on the whole (and only on the whole)—to link self-esteem with national status, although there may be marked class differences in this respect in persons from these areas. Those who do feel that their self-esteem is deeply invested in national status are taking an understandable and perhaps even realistic position. They may belong to a rising elite group in their country. They share with many of the new elite in their countries high aspirations for the growth and development of their homelands. Indeed, they may study abroad expressly to acquire techniques and skills that they hope to employ in the service of their homelands. They have experienced the new self-confidence and pride of peoples who have not always been treated with courtesy and respect. But also, and quite realistically, they hope that their personal careers will be intimately and importantly knit to the development of their countries. They see national growth and personal advancement as closely meshed. However, citizens of countries that have a slower rate of change, or citizens of countries where government, professions, and class distinctions are all more nearly in equilibrium, may on the whole (and only on the whole) be less inclined to identify self-esteem and national status.

Social revolutions and the attendant rise of a new elite do not occur with the same dramatic clarity in the older and more established nations of the world, and therefore individuals appraise their life situations accordingly. Opportunities at home for personal advancement are relatively limited. Life trajectories are more firmly predetermined. In this connection, one gets the impression that students from north European countries, for example, much less frequently present a picture of self-esteem involving national status. A careful study along these lines is needed and would have many interesting implications. The second phase of the research that is under way by the Social Science Research Council's Committee on Cross-Cultural Education should throw additional light on this subject and refine our understanding of it.

"Cultural Ambassadors."—In this connection, the term "cultural ambassador" or "unofficial ambassador" that has acquired popularity in some quarters warrants scrutiny. The term "unofficial ambassador" can have a very different meaning for an American whose education has been minimally influenced by government from its meaning for a foreigner whose education has been rigidly controlled by the central government. In the latter case, a study grant, whether from the home government or the United States, is inevitably given more official significance than it receives in the United States.

However, even the less-colored term "cultural ambassador" also can have interesting implications for role expectancies and status. If an individual conceives of himself as a "cultural ambassador," does he receive consistently, or inconsistently, treatment commensurate with the role in which he sees himself? And is that role perhaps realistic at home but not in the United States? An example is the case of a young Lebanese villager who studied at the American University of Beirut and then received a graduate fellowship to the United States. In terms of his fellow-villagers, his faculty advisers, and the binational selection committee, he had every reason to envisage himself as an outstanding man (which he was in his country) and to see his role as that of a national representative. He arrived on a Friday afternoon at the New York International Airport with about ten American dollars. His ear for American English was less acute than he had assumed. The customs officials were not deferential. A harassed secretary from an unknown organization hurriedly assisted him before setting out on her Long Island week end. He reached New York, wandered the streets, and finally was directed to a YMCA. There he remained until ten o'clock Monday morning when he was able to establish contact with the sponsoring agency. There he sat in line and waited until an overworked young woman hastily arranged his next steps.

The contrast between legitimate expectations and legitimate, if harsh, realities is the issue and not a judgment on any of the strands in the warp and weft of the particular case used for illustrative purposes. There are psychological hazards in the indiscriminate use of such a term as "cultural ambassador" or in overstating the importance of the grantee's mission and role. Within the limits of personal idiosyncrasies and allowing for a reasonable margin of error, the expectations involving self-esteem and national status can be predicted by a full and accurate prior knowledge of the student's home country (by Americans) and of the host country (by the visitor).

Discrimination.—Closely allied to the preceding discussion is the subject of race and discrimination. It is evident to all that if a student belongs to one of the dark-skinned peoples of the world, he faces in the United States both real and imagined problems of race relations. Further, it is unlikely that he will land in this country devoid of views on the subject. We in the United States are both vulnerable and sensitive on this issue, and this vulnerability has been exploited by both organized groups and individuals who view us, for varying reasons, with distrust and hostility. We are also not above reacting defensively. There is no intention here to go into the many difficult practical problems associated with racial discrimination as it affects foreign students in the United States. On the whole, one has the impression that our students, our educators, our officials, and many of our private citizens handle this subject constructively and with tact. For example, returns from 800 foreign students queried on this subject in 1952 revealed that nine out of ten felt that their American classmates received them on equal terms and without discrimination, and the large majority felt that they had also been well received by people outside the campus limits.[3]

However, discrimination is not based on the single or simple factor of skin color. For example, Mexican students, like most other foreign nationals, may deplore American race prejudices without ever encountering them. Mexican students in the colleges of our southwestern states do not generally identify themselves nor are they identified with those Mexican groups against whom discrimination is practiced in that region. The ethnic and class structure of Mexico will probably separate them, both in their own and in American awareness, from "braceros" or from "wetbacks." Similarly, Indians, whose skin color may be

---

[3] Edward C. Cieslak, "A Study of Administrative and Guidance Practices for Students from Abroad in Representative Collegiate Institutions of the U.S." (Mimeographed; Ph.D. dissertation, Dept. of Education, Wayne University, 1953), pp. 293–94.

dark, are frequently protected from discriminatory practices because of their obvious "foreignness." This does not prevent many Indian students from being among the most vehement critics of this aspect of American life. So, too, Scandinavians, who for the most part are cordially received in this country, may deplore American race relations but are usually without the emotional intensity that results from personal indignities.

In other words, it is necessary to distinguish between expectations, moral judgments, and experience. Probably relatively few foreign students have had personal experiences with the cruder varieties of racial discrimination. More suffer from difficulties of strangeness and communication than from difficulties created by active prejudice, and sensitive students may interpret social distance as racial discrimination. In addition, even those who have no occasion to experience discrimination personally or even to interpret social distance as such may pass stringent moral judgments on American race relations. Our own adverse reputation abroad on this score undoubtedly encourages our foreign visitors to react on this issue. In dealing with the individual student, it is helpful to know in what context he is reacting to racial and discriminatory issues and to realize that criticism may stem from objective moral judgments, from displaced feelings allied to strangeness and social distance, or from actual personal slights to the human dignity of a dark-skinned person.

In broader terms, expectations on the part of foreign students derive from the urgency of their personal ambitions and the validity, in their home environment, of their anticipated roles. If the host country, for equally valid and urgent reasons, fails to provide avenues to the expected goal or to sustain the anticipated role, at worst self-esteem may be irreparably damaged and at best adaptation to the United States may be off to an unfavorable start.

Once a foreign student's predeparture, adjustment, and readjustment problems are framed in terms of self-esteem, the way may be opened to sort out real difficulties from projective difficulties. For example, if a foreign student finds he cannot understand or speak English as well as he had thought, the damage may be more serious to his self-esteem than to his studies program, although his complaint may be about his studies and the quality of his instructor's speech. Or, to cite another example in positive terms, if a foreign student arrives with objective educational goals, his reactions to study abroad may be judged largely in terms of goal achievements rather than self-esteem. He will be concerned primarily with whether or not he has acquired the skills and assets relevant to his personal expectations. Under such circumstances his self-esteem may in certain cases be secure enough to compensate for a low accorded national status, racial discrimination, or a variety of situational difficulties, as long as his objective educational goals are constructively realized.

Throughout this volume, there will be many references both to self-esteem and to the distinction between real and projected difficulties. These are factors that cannot be adequately appraised or measured at this time, but awareness of them may serve to sharpen both administrative policies and individual counseling.

Firmness of Anchorage

The status of a foreign student's native country, whether felt or accorded is, of course, only one factor in the effect that nationality may have upon his set toward the host country. "Firmness of anchorage"—that is, the student's sense of clear purpose and of relatedness to his homeland—may affect the learning process in both its formal and informal aspects in the host country. Confusion about the direction and purpose of the home country because of a rapidly changing situation may produce weakness of anchorage in the home scene. The stability of the economic, social, and political institutions of the homeland may prove to be significant on several levels. One aspect of political stability was touched upon in the preceding paragraphs on national status and self-esteem in the discussion of students from colonial or recently colonial countries. But more broadly considered, any society that is experiencing rapid change is likely to produce psychological tensions among its individual members. It is often conducive to the creation of "marginal men" and to *anomie*.[4] In such cases, a person who goes abroad to study may be to some degree a variant or even a deviant in his own society. He may belong to a variant group that is the vanguard effecting on-going changes in his nation, and his membership in it may advance his life chances. But the position of a vanguard variant may be held at the cost of certain psychic strain. He may belong to a deviant group that may never be fully incorporated into the main stream of the national life; or he may belong to a group whose role in national life is approaching extinction.

Life Chances and Life Expectations.—Most students who go abroad for a period of study will see their sojourn in terms of gains expected from it. At a superficial level the student's life expectations may be enhanced by foreign study only in that within a social clique he may be considered traveled or culti-vated. At a more serious level a student may see himself contributing to the welfare of his nation, in whose leadership he hopes to play a significant role. In still other cases the student's hopes for the future are rooted in his chances for emigration. As used here "life chances" is a term in the realm of objective

[4] "Anomie" is a term introduced by Durkheim. The following definition is derived from Talcott Parsons, *Essays in Sociological Theory* (Rev. ed.; Glencoe, Ill.: Free Press, 1954), p. 125. "Anomie may perhaps most briefly be characterized as the state where large numbers of individuals are to a serious degree lacking in the kind of integration with stable institutional patterns which is essential to their own personal stability and to the smooth functioning of the social system."

social diagnosis, whereas "life expectations" relate to the individual's appraisal of his personal situation. In other words, life chances are to life expectations as national status is to felt national status. The difference between what appears to be objectively true and what is subjectively believed can be a vital determinant in any life trajectory. The opportunities that a foreign student sees for himself in his homeland will undoubtedly affect his reactions to a study sojourn in the United States. Objectively, nations differ in their ability to provide employment for their educated citizens. The competition for existing professional opportunities in the north European countries, for example, is acute. In certain fields, such as medicine, the competition for a livelihood in the "desirable" urban centers of India is also acute although the rural areas are recognized to be sadly in need of medical personnel. Almost any professional skill will contribute to the development of, and be rewarded in, Nigeria and Libya. But in any event it is useful to distinguish between life expectations and life chances and to realize that they may not always be objectively related to each other.

Life chances may be determined not only by the level of technical development in a nation, but also by many different and often subtle aspects of social structuring and of value systems. For example, in a society where the opportunity to exercise initiative is a function of hierarchical position, a young man may have no opportunity to use his foreign training until several years after his return and until he has acquired the status or age at which decision-making is allowed an individual in his culture. Considerations of this nature may well affect administrators' selections of persons to study abroad. They will presumably also affect the sense of satisfaction or frustration with study abroad that a young person feels on his return. For example, the political and economic conditions in postwar Germany and Austria have seriously encouraged the desire on the part of students from those countries to stay in the United

States rather than return home, whereas West African students are reported to be eager to return to their countries even after they may have spent several years in this country completing their studies.

Terms like "firmness of anchorage," "involvement in national status," and "life expectations" can be given certain interpretations stemming from depth psychology although the personality dynamics of people who are firmly anchored in their own culture is certainly not yet clearly understood. For instance, it has been suggested that a deep attachment to parents or a parental figure would tend to enhance an identification with community or nation.[5]

On a less speculative basis it seems legitimate to suggest that life chances and expectations are also closely related to primary and secondary group affiliations of individual students—in other words, to social class. A person who comes from the upper classes of a society and who already has some professional training and a position in a governmental, educational, or industrial hierarchy may have a clearly charted course ahead of him. His anchorage in the home scene is firm. His approach to a study period in the United States is likely to be quite rigidly defined in terms of what he needs for a future career, and his adjustment will be positive or negative to the degree that he is able to satisfy these aspirations. But a person from the same nation whose family may be without influence and who has not yet entered a life career is likely to see his life expectations in less positive and less precise terms.

But even an individual with a firm anchorage in the home scene may have to reassess his position during a foreign sojourn; if sudden changes occur at home during his absence, his life chances and expectations may be much reduced. The rise to power of a new political group or an economic setback at home

[5] Communication by a psychoanalyst consulted in relation to a foreign student who showed pathological disturbances.

may alter the student's position with respect to his homeland. Even objectively based life expectancies may then no longer coincide with life chances. The situation of literally thousands of Chinese students in the United States at the time the Chinese Communists came into power is a well-known and dramatic illustration of this situation.

The stability of national life and its relations to life chances and expectations cannot be overlooked. In a rapidly changing national life, there is the concomitant consideration that psychological stress may be greatest on just those segments of the population which are most likely to want to study abroad.

Cultural Distance

Presumably the set of a foreign student toward the host country will also be affected by his previous experience in cross-cultural contacts. The assumption made here is that either a living or an intellectual experience with other cultural or valuational constellations may develop, but does not necessarily assure, the tolerance and personal resilience conducive to cross-cultural adaptation.

The degree of social and cultural differences is also operative in such experiences (see also chapter 4, page 31). The cultural contrast between the United States and Canada may be considered minimal. Those between the United States and Italy are greater, and those between the United States and India greater still. However, complications are inherent in the concept of culture contrast when it is translated into individual terms. For example, a student from Bombay who goes to New Orleans may find the contrast in these two urban environments less marked than will a student who comes to New York City from an Anglo-Mexican community of the American Southwest.

Experience alone does not assure tolerance or personal resilience. It may actually so disturb certain personalities that it serves only to make them reinforce defensively the boundaries of their familiar world. In fact, some early findings suggest that precisely those individuals who lack direct experience with other cultures prior to arrival in the United States but who have had a relatively high number of prior although indirect contacts with America are inclined to react favorably to this country.[6]

Cultural contrast and previous cross-cultural experiences, like the other factors so far suggested, represent only a lead for investigation. They are factors whose range may be both wide and difficult to appraise and in which no one-to-one correlation can be assumed between experiences and individual modes of handling them. As an area of inquiry in attempting to understand forces influencing adjustment, it deserves far more careful consideration than is given it.

International Relations

So far, the factors enumerated have been largely those that operate within the framework of processes directly analyzable in people and their immediate social relations. However, the formal relationships between national governments may have dramatic symbolic influence on individual expectations and adjustments. That national stereotypes shift over time is well known; popular images of nations are as labile as positions in diplomatic debate. While such factors may operate significantly in the prearrival and sojourn sets of foreign students, perhaps more important is the effect such fluctuations may have on postreturn life chances.

Although political relations between home and host country may be of crucial importance in appraising the on-going life

[6] William H. Sewell and others, Project Staff at the University of Wisconsin, "A Preliminary Report on the Scandinavian Student Study," prepared for the Committee on Cross-Cultural Education of the Social Science Research Council, submitted Oct. 7, 1953 (Mimeographed), Section VI-B.

experience of an individual, their analysis belongs to a different "system of reality" from other factors so far suggested. They do not belong to "systems of reality" that either visitor or host is likely to be able to influence very directly. Therefore, attitude studies on a descriptive level and investigations of national stereotypes and opinions are not likely to have much permanence or much explicative value in understanding the processes of cross-cultural education.

Summary

In this section some of the predeparture factors that may affect a student's attitude, experience, and reaction toward the host country have been identified. Self-esteem has been taken as one of the key themes in this chapter. Questions of life chances and life expectancies as related to the firmness of anchorage in the home scene and the troublesome concept of culture contrasts and experience with such contrasts have been discussed. The political relations between home and host country cannot be ignored: their interaction is even more complex.

But whatever the web of sets and expectations a new arrival brings with him, he has still to achieve a relationship to the way of life of the country that is his host and to the particular situational experiences he will encounter.

Chapter **6**

SOME RELEVANT CONFIGURATIONS OF AMERICAN LIFE

Iɴ ᴛʜᴇ behavior and attitudes of social aggregates and in the formal and informal institutions, certain coherences can be discovered that have been given various designations—patterns, themes, values, and configurations. These configurations serve to bring into meaningful relationships what seem to be unrelated materials on social life. Frequently the very individuals who live within the framework of such patterns are unable to recognize them consciously or are unaware of their full scope. The reasons for such myopia are not far to seek. Members of a given group have from birth onward been steadily taught both by direct and indirect methods to acquire such patterns. This is, of course, the process of enculturation which transforms every unsocialized infant into a more or less socialized representative of his group. To the individual, his behavior, his values, and his social milieu are "perfectly natural" and represent "human nature." Much of that great reservoir of learned behavior and of attitudes is taken so much for granted that it is relegated to the habitual and to the subconscious.

It is little wonder, therefore, that a trained foreign observer can often sense the arbitrary but coherent pattern of a society more clearly than can a member of the group itself, but at the same time he may be quite unaware of his own "perfectly natural" blind spots. In any event, comparisons are the essence of cross-cultural experiences. A person who faces a culture foreign to him draws comparisons between it and his own group, and objective insights become possible only as channels of communication are opened. Every foreign student is faced more or less consciously with the task of appraising the host country and the people he meets there in terms of the comparative perspectives his background provides him.

Ever since the establishment of the American nation, foreign observers have left records of their impressions of the quality and direction of our national life. One of the early and most prescient of these observers was Alexis de Tocqueville. Since De Tocqueville's day, many foreign observers have contributed to this vast literature on American life, and more recently American scholars have attempted to see their culture with objectivity, using the tools of social anthropology and comparative sociology. More pertinent for our purposes, foreign students reveal remarkable consistencies in the comments they make on those aspects of American life that strike them most forcibly.

The comments which follow have been shaped by observations of social philosophers, social scientists, and particularly the numerous, unsystematized impressions of foreign students in the postwar period. Only those patterns have been selected that seem to bear most closely on our relations with, and handling of, foreign students. It is not a "national character" description nor a systematic survey and analysis of all of American culture. It is not the whole story of American life nor a description of any one American.

The propositions advanced are of differing orders of generality and of differing validity, and the claims made for what follows are, therefore, modest. The intent is to present materials that clarify certain practical and human situations and provoke more thoughtful formulations by those who deal with foreign students in the United States.

Clyde and Florence Kluckhohn have provided a singularly useful concept of one of the values of American life; it is termed by them the effort-optimism syndrome. They introduce their discussion of this trait in the following words:

> No conversational bromides are more characteristically American than "Let's get going"; "Do something"; "Something can be done about it." Although during the thirties there was widespread devaluation of present and future and, though pessimism and apathy about the atomic bomb and other international problems are certainly strong currents in contemporary thinking, the dominant American reaction is still—against the perspective of other cultures—that this is a world in which effort triumphs.[1]

The high value placed in this country on effort and its presumed rewards is manifest in our attitude toward work. Work is a virtue. If at first we don't succeed, we are inclined to redouble our efforts rather than pause to take thought. Also, more than most nations we respect all kinds of work. On the one hand we do not attach the same degree of prestige to mental work that many societies do; on the other hand, manual labor is not considered demeaning as it is in many societies. The suggestion to foreign students that they wait on tables or do other kinds of "menial" work to supplement income while studying can present a difficult hurdle to certain of them. The egalitarian strand in American life—to be discussed presently—makes itself felt in the realm of work.

This characteristic is summarized in the comments of foreign visitors when they speak of our youthfulness, when they comment on our preoccupation with work and the dignity we attach

[1] Clyde Kluckhohn and Florence R. Kluckhohn, "American Culture: Generalized Orientations and Class Patterns," *Conflicts of Power in Modern Culture* ed. Lyman Bryson, Louis Finkelstein, and R. M. MacIver (New York: Harper & Bros., 1947).

to it, when they say that we are doers (activists). If a certain negative affect is associated with such observations, it can be phrased in less flattering language. Thus, youthfulness can be called immaturity. Our preoccupation with activity may be interpreted as superficiality and shallowness and is perceived as the antithesis of intellectuality and contemplation. Visitors to this country during periods in American history when the anti-intellectuals (the anti- "long hair" and "egg-head" periods) have been in vocal political positions can marshal considerable evidence for such negative judgments.

Consistent with the effort-optimism syndrome and its associated activism is the tradition of citizen participation. This is not, either as an institution or as a value, unique to the United States. Rather, it is the underlying philosophy of Western democracy. But that it is not a universal value is illustrated by the rather petulant comment of a sophisticated Indian farmer who closed a discussion concerning the establishment of a clinic in his village with the comment, "Well, if the government won't help us, why should we help ourselves?" Whatever the historical roots and philosophic justification for such a position in India, it is antithetic to the American position of citizen participation and responsibility with the attendant sociocentrism.

This apparently simple statement leads to a series of complicated considerations. The United States may not be the nation in which such sociocentric values have the most extreme expression, but to students from many lands they are strikingly developed in the United States. To nationals of countries where loyalty centers in families and/or cliques, this type of identification with national symbols can be a troublesome idea. The ramifications of an attachment to "the rights of fellow-citizens" may seem to the visitor ludicrously unrealistic compared to the obligations one owes a person known face to face and perhaps related by blood ties.

Such an attachment may seem equally grotesque to foreign

students whose center of values lies in the cultivation of in-dividualism. In other words, even the moderate sociocentrism operative in the United States may startle, for different reasons, those individuals rooted in societies that prize familistic and clique ties and those individuals rooted in societies where in-dividualism is prized.

This leads inevitably to another distinction that is not always apparent to Americans. In a certain sense no society prizes more than our own the individual—defined as a biological entity. On the other hand, the United States is not pre-eminent in its cultivation of individualism: it does not, for example, value the development of each person's uniqueness to the degree cus-tomary in a nation like France. Unless the distinction between prizing the individual and the cultivation of individualism is borne clearly in mind by Americans themselves, we may not be in a position to understand the confusion on this score that foreign students often experience.

Linked to American sociocentrism is still another series of considerations. If a nation is dedicated to a commonweal that is phrased in terms of a citizenry in whom power is vested ultimately, then there is urgent need for an educated electorate. In the United States this has resulted in an educational system obligated to provide its citizenry not only with elementary skills essential to its technology, but also with the capacity for sophis-ticated judgments on complex sociopolitical issues. The result has been to prolong education for increasing numbers of the population. In the process, many people now believe that in the undergraduate colleges, at least, quantity is being emphasized rather than quality. Depending upon the comparisons that foreign students bring to bear on this dilemma in American life, they either admire the proliferation of the educational system or deplore its quality, its rigidity of point systems and class attendance. In education there emerges again one aspect of the effort-optimism theme. We tend to assume that if enough people diligently attend college and make the necessary work effort, we shall achieve a citizenry capable of making intelligent decisions as voters and capable of carrying out the work that our sociocentric goals set us—"the greatest good to the greatest number," "the rising standard of living," the idea of progress with its (optimistically) expanding universe. To young foreign students from countries that are relatively stabilized such as the Scandinavian countries, or relatively traditional as Thailand, or relatively underprivileged economically as Syria, such values may be seductive but their immediate applicability to their homelands will not be obvious.

Another aspect of American life and values that repeatedly impresses visitors from abroad is the tradition of egalitarianism. Over one hundred and twenty-five years ago De Tocqueville suggested that Americans are more interested in equality than liberty. Associated with this attitude is the distrust in American society of hierarchically structured authority. Although in a republic we must obviously delegate power, there is a strong tendency toward "checks and balances." This process operates in more than our formal government organization. Any prominent leader must be prepared to be vigorously attacked in proportion to the power he wields. The very informality and rapid first-name basis on which we conduct both business and social relations are further symptoms of an unwillingness and hesitancy in assuming or in recognizing a hierarchically superior status. The cordial interpersonal relationships of American life are frequently noted and almost invariably approved by foreign students. But the social informality that implies our distrust of authority and status can be disconcerting to visitors who come from societies that accord at least outward respect to high status and that express respect in formal behavior.

On campuses, foreign students are almost always astonished by the informal and casually friendly relations that prevail between professors and students. Rarely does the first astonishment associated with such observations crystallize into a negative judgment, and it appears that this American pattern of interpersonal relations is usually approved and often assimilated in the course of the sojourn in the United States. There is some indication, however, that these patterns of egalitarian interpersonal relations may cause some readjustment hazards if and when they are transplanted by students returning to more formal, hierarchical societies.

However, easy cordiality may lead those who are unaccustomed to our mores into overestimating the depth and intent of our social gestures. There was the case, for example, of the young foreign student introduced at a tea to the president of the college in which he had just registered. The president's "I am glad to see you here—how are you" was interpreted as a sign of personal concern which had subsequently to be somewhat painfully corrected. Part of the error of interpretation lay in the fact that the young foreigner belonged to a superior family and felt that his status warranted more than the egalitarian treatment meted out to him. Malaise resulting from such egalitarian treatment of individuals can be given the negative interpretation of a certain lack of sensitivity to individual differences. Stereotyped counseling, books on how to make friends and influence people, and superficial friendliness may all serve to reinforce such impressions. They may then be phrased as more general condemnations of "American mass society," "individuals as units," and the "manipulated and mechanical quality of American life."

Once a visitor with negative emotional reactions toward his American sojourn accepts the interpretations of American life as mechanical, it is only a step further to see it also as materialistic. We need scarcely be told that this is one of the most common stereotypes current about the United States. The material wealth we have at our disposal tends to confirm this opinion. Less often is it realized that our wealth is a combination of rich continental resources and of the effort-optimism syndrome, with the associated belief in the virtue of work. And certainly many visitors here discover with some astonishment that we are in fact a people who work extremely hard. They discover that wealth does not connote for us the opportunity for pursuing leisure that may be prized in their own society or social group.

The theme of our frank, informal egalitarian tradition has led us back again into the work and activism motive. It might just as easily have been meshed into the subject of friendship which is so often a source of bewilderment to foreign students. To many peoples our casual warmth, our easy egalitarianism, connotes an offer of friendship that may not be intended. As many foreign students have said, "Americans are friendly but do not have true friendships." However, what constitutes the friendship relationship and its expectations appears to be, in part at least, culturally determined. There exists, to my knowledge, no adequate comparative exploration of this theme.[2] This is regrettable because it promises to be a rewarding one, since the establishment of warm supportive interpersonal relationships appears to be a crucial element in the adjustment of foreign students. At this stage the guess may be hazarded that friendships vary from culture to culture with respect to spread, obligations, duration, and mutual trust. Friendship also seems to vary from culture to culture in the importance assigned it in the hierarchy of interpersonal relations. If one were to characterize comparatively United States friendship patterns with respect to these four factors, one would say that they are widespread, low in obligations, short in duration, and high in trust. Obviously high and low can be used in relation only to some scale. No such scale exists. Yet, comparing American and Japanese friendship

[2] The writer presented a fuller but still far from adequate discussion of this theme called "Cultural Factors in the Psychological Counseling of Foreign Students" at the University of Minnesota Institute on Counseling Foreign Students, Jan. 19, 1954 (Unpublished MS).

patterns, for example, one might characterize the latter as small in spread, high in obligation, long in duration, and high in trust. The social configurations emerging from even such a casual comparison are obvious. If friendships in the United States are wide and low in obligation, they will be easily sought out, and broad social relations (egalitarianism) are readily opened up. It can be only within such a cultural context that a foreign student adviser is urged to be "a real friend"[3] to students from abroad. One is tempted to speculate on the disappointment and sense of failure a counselor experiences when his well-meant but ethnocentric approach encounters, for example, the Japanese pattern of friendship, restricted in number and heavily obligated. Thus, in contacts with Japanese, caution must be exercised in entering into such relationships, and facile fraternizing is not to be anticipated.

In Mexico, still another configuration seems to emerge. Friendship as such ranks below kinship in the order of human relationships. If friendship exists, it is in terms of special relations to real (or putative) kin. This justifies obligations and overcomes the suspicion and the short-term quality of clique relationships.

Obviously, our friendship patterns may affect foreign students in this country deeply and in areas of considerable sensitivity. Our good intentions may be perceived and appreciated, but they need not necessarily produce the reactions we anticipate. Our "friendliness" may appear to be a tactless intrusion upon highly cherished reserve. The Chinese student who is asked to tell about some personal experience in addressing the Rotary Club instead of speaking about Ming ceramics may be aware of our amiable motives but may, nevertheless, feel that the request is lacking in tact and a decent regard for human dignity as he envisages it.

[3] National Association of Foreign Student Advisers, *Handbook for Counselors of Students from Abroad* (Experimental ed.; New York: The Association, n.d.), pp. 124, 135–36 provide a good example of this sort of well-meaning but ethnocentric advice.

We have alluded so far to a series of strands that are tightly interwoven in the fabric of American life. Of these, certain ones —citizen responsibility, material wealth, egalitarianism, and the wide spread of friendships—can all be subsumed under a widely accepted opinion about Americans. They are generous. But here again we face serious comparative issues. The giving-receiving relationship is differently structured in different societies. Again, we lack any adequate comparative study. And again we are forced, as in the case of "friendship," to a few isolated cases that may suggest the richness of the typologies.

Let us assume that in the United States generosity is a self-enhancing activity and that it entails no more than a loosely structured obligation to gratitude in return. India appears to present an interesting contrast. Insofar as one may risk any generalization about so heterogeneous a nation, in India giving is largely the obligation of the privileged. Receiving is the due of the less-privileged. Gratitude is not involved since the privileged gain in merit by giving. In practical terms, the less-privileged are concerned with manipulating the privileged to assure that they do not falter in either temporal or eternal obligations. The position of the Indian student, who opens an interview by saying "The United States is rich and India is poor," has established a relationship pattern that Americans are slow to recognize. Americans, with their egalitarian traditions and their distrust of authority, are likely to protest such a categorization of the two countries. The Indian student may see such a protest as evasion of obligation and as a cue to manipulate, persistently, the "reality" as he sees it.

However invalid the foregoing speculations may prove to be, they serve as preliminary examples of the kinds of misunderstanding about values that can arise between people who are rooted in different cultural systems with their attendant but often unformulated expectations. Foreign students are not only faced with the necessity of understanding and adjusting to

American values; they are also, on a more specific level, faced with adapting to them as they are manifested in the expectations that Americans invest in foreign students.

For the time being, it is possible only to jot down a few random observations and impressions. For example, Americans who deal with foreign students do not escape the frustration and hostilities attendant upon cross-cultural contacts. Failure on the part of a foreign student to keep to carefully laid plans, to manage his funds efficiently, to "appreciate what has been done for him," or to fail to admire the United States are frequent subjects of conversations in which an underlying acrimony is often detectable. Many Americans also expect of foreign students a "quaintness," an entertainment quality, which, if lacking, leaves a sense of having been let down. There are American students who invest in compensatory friendships with foreign students in an attempt to right the balance of their own maladjustments to the American scene and who find in association with foreign students the same escapist satisfactions that some foreign students find in coming to the United States.

Thus, the American scene, like every other cultural entity, presents valuational and relational situations to foreign guests that are not necessarily obvious to them. Perhaps one of the greatest practical contributions that orientation work and student counseling can stress is an understanding of American culture in these terms.

Chapter 7

STAGES OF ADJUSTMENT AND READJUSTMENT

So FAR consideration has been given to a variety of factors that appear to have significance in the attitudes or sets that students from other countries bring with them to the United States. Some of the relevant American interpersonal relationships and values that they encounter have been suggested. Upon arrival adjustment between the student's sets and the American actualities begins to take place. It is helpful to postulate tentatively certain phases in both the adjustment processes here and in the readjustment processes upon return to the homeland. That they are roughly analogous to the stages in psychiatric treatment has been suggested. Or, as one perceptive person once remarked, "If you live in a country three months, you love it; if you live in it for a year, you hate it; if you live in it two years, you are used to it."

It may be useful to repeat that the steps suggested here have been assigned neither value judgments nor absolute time spans. Obviously the time required for an individual to pass through a series of adjustment and readjustment phases will be a function of many complex, interlocking factors. Similarly, the "qual-

66

ity" of adjustment made can be determined only in a comparable way. These phases are not sharply demarcated and certain vacillations may be assumed to exist in the sequences suggested here.

The adjustive processes can be broken down into four phases: the spectator, the adaptive, the "coming to terms," and the predeparture.[1]

The Spectator Phase

The spectator phase [2] is "characterized by psychological detachment from the new experience. Things 'happen to' the visitor which he notes as expected, strange or novel. While the experience may be 'interesting,' 'exciting,' 'confusing' or even 'humiliating,' the visitor is protected from serious distress or major influence since he is not yet personally involved in the new scene."

This period may last until the first task or the first role as a participant in the American scene is undertaken. In the case of relatively short leadership and visitor tours, a nonparticipant spectator role may characterize the individual's attitude throughout the sojourn. In the cases of certain individuals such as journalists, trained social scientists with specialization in the American scene, or important political leaders, the spectator role may persist throughout even a prolonged sojourn.

During the spectator period the stresses of adjustment are assumed to exist primarily in the more superficial aspects of the personality. For example, considerable nervous fatigue may result from the frustrations involved in neither fully understanding nor being able to express oneself in an unfamiliar language,

[1] The writer is particularly indebted to Mr. Brewster Smith of the Social Science Research Council's Committee on Cross-Cultural Education for much of the phrasing used to described these phases. Many phrases have been used verbatim from his memorandum of Nov. 19, 1953, to the committee.

[2] Lippitt has called this the "stranger phase."

or from efforts to catch the cues essential to courteous behavior in a strange society. But the individual's psychological economy, although taxed, is not threatened by such stresses.

The Adaptive Phase

The adaptive phase [3] is "characterized by active involvement in the problem of adjustment to the life of the host country. Adjustive stresses become prominent and the visitor tries out his repertory of adjustive strategies and tactics." This is the period during which the individual first begins to participate in American culture, when he enters upon set tasks that require adaptation to American institutions, and when he becomes emotionally engaged in the network of values, customs, and habits prevalent in this country. During this period the adjustment stresses, whether minor or major in intensity, are felt most acutely.

There is some indication that if personal contacts with Americans are freely sought during the spectator phase, there may be some withdrawal to groups of fellow-nationals or to other foreign students during the adaptive phase. The reason suggested for such withdrawal, if it occurs, is that inherent in the adaptive phase are the first serious threats to the individual's self-respect and his capacities to cope with situations that are charged with deep meaning for him. He may in the face of such threats seek more secure and familiar, and therefore less threatening, relationships. This is a nonpathological manifestation of the familiar ego-defense mechanism that depth psychologists term "regression."

The foregoing reasoning suggests that if a sojourn is cut short during the adaptive phase, negative reactions are likely to color the recall of the host country because the sojourn has been cut off during precisely the period of unresolved conflict, when the

---

[3] Lippitt has called this the "learner phase."

so-called "culture shock" may be most acute. Similarly, it follows that if a brief spectator sojourn is so planned that it facilitates the loss of the spectator role and plunges the individual into participation in various United States–centered tasks, but is not long enough to permit opportunities to "come to terms" with the American scene, defensive reactions are encouraged but left unresolved. In any event, it seems likely that the intensity of the defensiveness will be in part a function of the difficulty that the individual feels participative roles and tasks impose on him.

The "Coming to Terms" Phase

The "coming to terms" phase sets in when the adaptive issues raised for the individual during the preceding phase are brought into an equilibrium. This period may be characterized by either marked positive or negative attitudes or by objective judgments of the host country. If the equilibrium is charged with negative affect toward the host country, overt criticisms and verbal aggressiveness may be more freely expressed than in the earlier phases.

In this connection two particularly interesting articles are available. Norman Kiell [4] published a brief study on the attitudes of Indian students [5] toward the United States in which the following statement dismayed many people.

But after spending some time here—an average of fifteen months—the students have opinions which indicate that for the majority disillusionment and disappointment have colored their experience. The figures illustrate the downward curve of their approval. Before arrival here, 68 percent had markedly favorable opinions of the

[4] Kiell, "Attitudes of Foreign Students," *Journal of Higher Education,* XXII (1951), 189.

[5] Dr. Kiell in the article quoted above does not specify that the subjects are Indian students but a reference to his unpublished thesis indicates that this national group served as his subjects.

United States;[6] after they had been here a short while, 89 percent thought well of their host nation. But after living here from four to forty months only 22 percent were still favorably inclined in their attitudes to the United States. Fifty-seven percent held decidedly unfavorable opinions. An additional 21 percent had "mixed" views, which means that the favorable impressions dwindled from 89 percent to 22 percent between the time the students had their first glimpse of this country and the time they were interviewed.

If the idea of phases had been used in connection with this study, if reliance had not been placed upon recalled attitudes, and if we were given a more refined breakdown of favorable, unfavorable, and mixed views, the implication of the foregoing quotation would probably be very different. Another study [7] that was pursued with greater sophistication serves to throw considerable light, along with the author's dynamic interpretations, on the actual processes of attitude changes in foreign students over a period of time. Forty Indian students were used as subjects. They were divided into a short-residence group (less than six months) and a long-residence group (more than six months but less than two years). They were given two questionnaires, one of which tested the need to conform and difficulty in conformity and, the second, the degree of attitudinal aggression.[8] Mr. Zajonc uses the sociological concept of role and the psychological concept of frustration and aggression. A foreign visitor must to some extent conform to the norms of the host culture, but because the student's personality equilibrium stems from another culture, conformity to a new pattern may prove disturbing often in deeply unconscious levels of his superego. The expressed difficulties may often be only superficial rationalizations of much deeper and often unconscious threats to the individual's equilibrium. He is forced

---

[6] This prearrival opinion is presumably based on recall whose reliability is perhaps questionable.

[7] Robert B. Zajonc, "Aggressive Attitudes of the 'Stranger' as a Function of Conformity Pressures," *Human Relations*, V (1952), 205–16.

[8] *Ibid.*, p. 210.

more or less consciously to recognize and to reweigh his original values, habits and beliefs, behaviors and attitudes.

However, the foreigners usually "occupy a uniquely endowed role in the host society." They enjoy, compared to their hosts, certain exemptions from conformity. Also as persons often considered endowed with a certain amount of objectivity, the visitors' opinions and judgments about the host country may even be solicited. "Even if he rejects or criticizes . . . he will seldom face punishment as a consequence."

A foreigner "who experiences pressures to conform and cannot, for some reason or another, is subject to frustration." He may express himself in aggressiveness. And the expression of such aggressiveness is facilitated by the very immunities of his role as a stranger. But the newly arrived stranger only gradually feels the pressures to conform and gradually learns the immunities of his role as a stranger. Therefore, some foreign students may become increasingly and overtly more disapproving and aggressive.

This study of Mr. Zajonc, excellent as it is, does not pretend to cover the full adjustive range of foreign students or describe their only reactive patterns. Also it need scarcely be stressed that the need to conform differs among individuals and that the sensitivity and insecurity attendant upon conformity pressures will vary greatly. It is even possible that there will be differences between national groups in this respect. Certainly the more a student feels the need to conform and the more he manifests insecurity, the greater is his need not only for favorable experiences but also for *consistently* favorable experiences. A foreign student who finds his sojourn in the United States relatively unthreatening and constructive may be expected to develop realistic (as opposed to wishful, projective, or defensive) appraisals of the host country. His opinion will then presumably belong to what Kiell called "mixed" views. Such a student is also likely to have positive affect toward the host country, or at least to recall the host country after his return with positive affect. Lastly, it may be postulated that the goals of such a student will expand during his sojourn.

However, a foreign student who finds his sojourn in the United States threatening to his personal equilibrium, or damaging to his self-esteem, will react with one or more of the familiar ego-defense mechanisms. He may become more overtly aggressive as was the case in Mr. Zajonc's study. This may be associated with the development of chauvinistic views. Most of us when exposed to an unfamiliar culture have experienced how easy it is to shift from tolerant patriotism to chauvinism. But a foreign student may also react with depression and withdrawal and often seek out the buttressing support of a group of fellow-nationals. He may engage in compensatory but not necessarily adaptive strivings in which he redoubles his work efforts and "works himself to death." He may even in some cases strive to identify with the very source of threat and become "more American than the Americans."

All learning entails anxiety—although presumably not of the neurotic variety in most instances. But ways of coping with anxiety will vary greatly between individuals, for there may also be culturally preferred channels for the expression of anxiety. For example, overt aggression seems more common to Americans and Indians, whereas Indonesians may more frequently express anxiety in withdrawal and depression. Although each culture may have more or fewer institutional outlets for tension, the culture alone does not determine how each individual will cope with his insecurities, particularly when he is abroad.

The foregoing discussion presents only the most preliminary suggestions concerning psychological processes. They may offer a small degree of insight into the manner in which foreign students adapt to, and come to terms with, the host country.

The Predeparture Phase

The predeparture phase sets in shortly before the individual leaves the host country. The importance of returning home gains a new ascendancy in the awareness of the individual. He may look toward home with expectancy or apprehension, and he may attempt to prepare the way by renewing contacts with the homeland if they have been allowed to lapse during the sojourn abroad. It may also be assumed that during this phase he sees the host country and the sojourn period with a somewhat altered perspective.

Readjustment Phases

Upon return to his home country the individual who has studied abroad may again face a series of readjustments to his interpersonal relations, to the social changes that may have occurred during his absence, and to his life chances. All the former threads of his life will presumably be seen in a perspective which his sojourn abroad will have altered more or less deeply. Unfortunately, there are even fewer meaningful observations on this process than there are on the sojourn period. Nevertheless, at least three broad and schematic phases can be tentatively suggested that parallel those of the foreign sojourn: (1) the greetings and comparisons phase; (2) the stage of adapting and redefining personal relations and life chances; and (3) the "coming to terms" phase with the home country. For this last phase a certain gross typology can be suggested: (*a*) return to national norms; (*b*) acceptance of the role as a variant or a deviant;[9] (*c*) the assumption of permanent ambivalences and re-evaluations; and (*d*) alienation.

Certain preliminary studies amplify and partially substantiate

---

[9] By variant is meant recognized and permissible roles but not those given dominant value in the society. Variant roles may be complementary to dominant ones. By deviant is meant roles that may arouse varying degrees of censure or nonrecognition and consequent marginality in the society.

the typologies suggested here. Dr. O. W. Riegel's unpublished manuscript on Belgians who had studied in the United States [10] reports that "interest in and appreciation for the American way of life and American democracy tend to fall away with age, and with the remoteness of the American exchange experience." Politically among Belgian returnees there is no marked disposition, in general, to favor the American position more than the average Belgians do. However, it should be noted that the popularity of Americans is *not* synonymous with the popularity of the United States government. Four out of five Belgians who studied in the United States consider themselves more friendly toward Americans as a result of their sojourn here. This holds even for those who disagree with United States policies, who profited little from their educational experience in the United States, or who found the United States culturally barren. However, these judgments must be seen in the light of the general favorableness toward both the United States and Americans in Belgium. The United States ranked only after France in popularity at the time of the study in 1950. This may be an appropriate place to point out that, although the distinction between Americans and the policies of the United States government is a valid one, a favorable opinion of Americans may affect positively the motives that foreigners impute to unpopular government policies.

Further implications of Riegel's study are that Belgians who have studied in the United States approximate their national norm in political judgments about the United States and are only slightly more favorably disposed than their countrymen toward Americans as people. This finding coincides with re-

[10] This study by Riegel was made in Belgium during the summer of 1950 under the auspices of the Woodrow Wilson School of Public and International Affairs at Princeton. Dr. Riegel was kind enough to permit the writer to go over his two-volume manuscript report. For a published statement see: Riegel, "Residual Effects of Exchange of Persons," *Public Opinion Quarterly*, Fall 1953, pp. 319–27.

search on attitude changes in which it is found that the effect of a stimulus tapers off in the course of time.

On the other hand, Riegel's study also raises another interesting issue that throws light on the postulated "alienation" type of readjustment. He found that the desire to emigrate to the United States seems to be one of the more important results of the American study sojourn. Again, however, this must be seen in the context of the fact that 41 percent of all Belgians would prefer to live in some other country if they were financially free to choose their place of residence. It seems unlikely that the desire to emigrate always and necessarily represents psychological alienation from one's own country. It may mean no more than a realistic appraisal of life chances in the home country as opposed to a foreign country. Certainly one should not make a facile equation between alienation from one's own nation and the desire to emigrate. Similarly the distinction between alienation from one's own society and assimilation into another can by no means be equated. An alienated (denationalized) individual may never assimilate elsewhere and may live out his life as a variant wherever he resides.

Just as alienation, emigration, and assimilation cannot be equated, it may be useful to underline that many societies allow for different kinds of quite satisfactory roles as variants. If an individual's role as a variant is in the direction of social change, he may find himself increasingly in a leadership position. This was the experience of many Japanese liberals during the American occupation of Japan. Also, it may be necessary to remind Americans that in some societies large areas of reward are not withheld from deviants.

The returning student may face either the problem of "my place is no longer available," or "my place is still here but I no longer feel at ease in it, but there are other roles for me to assume." In the former case, the individual may feel no rejection but sees no opportunities. In the latter case, his reactions may range from constructive discontent with his lot to rejection of his native milieu.

In whatever way individuals may come to terms with their home country after a foreign sojourn, there are certain generalizations of these processes that may be advanced and that warrant future research. First, if the returned student's readjustment is in terms of reassuming national norms but if the prevalent attitude in the home country is one of suspicion or even hostility to the United States, one would expect the returnee to express a protective anti-Americanism. Stated in more general and slightly different terms, it is possible to propose that: (1) the effects of experiences are cumulative over time if they coincide with the existing attitudes of the subject and his reference group, and, conversely, (2) the effects of experiences taper off after a period of time if they are at variance with the existing attitudes of the subject and his reference group. It follows from the foregoing that the conflict aroused in individuals during their stay in the United States is not necessarily predictive of an overtly positive or negative attitude toward the United States upon return home. On the other hand, passive or highly adaptive (the "bending bamboo") reactions to the host country during the sojourn seem linked with the ready acceptance of formerly held norms upon return.

In this chapter, stress has been placed on the foreign study sojourn as only an episode in the individual's life. He reaches this country with certain attitudes about it and certain expectations. On meeting the realities of the American scene, including patterns of interpersonal relationships, he makes certain adjustments between his past conditioning, his present situation, and his long-run view of himself in relation to his homeland. Tentatively, the on-going adaptation has been broken down into four phases in the United States: the spectator, the adaptive, the "coming to terms," and the predeparture. Equally tentatively three phases of postreturn adjustment have been suggested:

greetings and comparisons, redefinition of role, and "coming to terms" with home country. This last phase may represent several kinds of solution, from a return to national norms to alienation. It must be stressed that this apparently orderly sequence awaits empiric validation. To the degree that it may have validity, it should be applied but with the utmost caution in any individual case.

Chapter 8

FACTORS IN SOJOURN ADJUSTMENT

I<small>N THE</small> search for generalized guides to factors that promote or inhibit adjustments to the host country during a period of study abroad, the anthropologically-minded (whether lay or professional) are likely to suggest that the greater the culture contrast between home and host country, the greater will be the severities of adjustments and the longer will be the time required to make them. Also, if a favorable adjustment entails a positive feeling toward the host country, the greater is the risk of alienation from the homeland. There is undoubtedly a certain validity in such suggestions. However, "culture contrast" is a concept that is only descriptive, although terminal. It risks placing the cart before the horse if one is concerned with the analysis of situations or individual reactions to them. When one uses the notion of culture contrast, one is faced with the almost insurmountable task (at this stage of social science development) of listing all the values, behavioral systems, and institutions in the United States as compared with those of 70 or 80 foreign countries. One is faced additionally with the complex problem of a measure of cultural distance.

For the time being it may, therefore, be desirable to try tools that are more sharply analytic than the concept of culture contrast. For example, the acceptance of, or resistance to, elements in the host culture will vary, depending on whether they represent areas in which individuals have: (1) firm emotional commitments (for example, paternal authority in the family or the indignity of physical labor); or (2) unresolved problems that the foreign experience activates (for instance, one's social status as a woman or the possibility of upward social mobility); or (3) no established positions, so that the new experiences are neither negatively nor positively affect-ladened (for example, the custom of group discussions or the pattern of informal social relationships across class lines).

Additionally and perhaps somewhat obviously we would expect acceptance of the host society to be high: (1) if the study experience meets the individual's expectations (for example, the acquisition of relevant skills or knowledge); and (2) if traits rejected by the foreign student in his own society (for example, widespread political corruption) are not found in the host society.

But we may also expect that resistance to the host society will be high: (1) if it threatens his self-esteem and associated prestige values (for example, the prestige accorded scholars); (2) if drastic changes in basic habits are required (for example, the inaccessibility of sex outlets); (3) if definite psychological commitments are required that the individual is not prepared to give (for example, anticommunism or pro-Americanism).

Quite apart from these broad suggestions about the emotional sets that affect acceptance of, or resistance to, elements in the host culture there is also a series of both mediating and situational factors that affect a foreign student's relations to the United States. Only some of the more salient are selected for discussion in the following paragraphs.

But before turning to these factors, a brief summary of what a group of foreign students reported on their own experiences may be of interest. Unfortunately, the phrasing of the questionnaire more or less predetermined the categories of responses received and to that extent they must be used with caution.

In March 1952 the Institute of International Education received 1,042 replies to a questionnaire that had been sent out to Department of State grantees who were in their first year of study in the United States. Information on a number of subjects was deliberately elicited, including housing arrangements, language difficulties, and so forth. In addition, however, a more open-ended question was asked concerning adjustment, namely, "Most persons have problems of adjustment when visiting a new country. What particular difficulties, if any, have you experienced in adjusting to the culture or customs of the United States which might have been avoided if you had been better informed?" [1]

Certainly, neither a written questionnaire of this type nor the limitation suggested by the clause ". . . might have been avoided if you had been better informed," nor the courtesy of most recipients of governmental grants, nor the possibility that some adjustment difficulties may be unconscious, lead one to suppose that either a full or clear story of the areas of adjustment problems of foreign students has been elicited. Nevertheless, as one of the few quantitative approaches to this matter, the analysis of replies is worth recapitulating.

Of the 1,042 respondents, 29 percent (or 298 respondents) cited one or more difficulties, 6 percent stated that adjustment problems were unavoidable; 44 percent said they had no adjustment problems; and 21 percent failed to answer. For the 298 respondents who reported difficulties of adjustment, the principal categories listed were: "Practical living problems" (31 percent, or 93 respondents); United States way of life, society, customs, etc. (25 percent, or 74 respondents); United States educational

---

[1] Bureau of Social Science Research, American University, *An Analysis of First Reports from Foreign Exchange Students: Academic Year 1951– 52,* prepared for the Educational Exchange Service, IIA, Dept. of State (Dittoed; Washington, March 1953), pp. 16 ff.

system (25 percent, or 73 respondents); English language (17 percent, or 49 respondents); opportunities for social contacts (9 percent, or 26 respondents); specific educational institutions (4 percent, or 13 respondents).

The material then is analyzed in an attempt to discover relationships between a "morale" code and sources of information available to the foreign student. For our purposes, perhaps the most revealing statement that emerges is that: "A sense of knowing where to go for advice appears to be a significant factor in the ease with which exchange students resolve certain types of adjustment problems; and informal, personal sources of advice would seem to be no less important than institutional sources." [2] As the authors point out, "One grantee may experience a difficulty as a 'problem'; another may not think of it as such. A problem quickly and satisfactorily solved by getting the right advice may be different from one that continues to plague the grantee during his entire stay." [3] This conclusion, emerging from a frame of reference different from that employed in the present analysis, clearly underlines the importance of good interpersonal relations for the adjustment of foreign students.

Language Facility

The importance of interpersonal relations as well as the importance of the whole formal educational process will be mediated by the ability to communicate. Language, therefore, is a factor of primary importance in the sojourn adjustment.

Of the 1,042 first-year foreign students in 1951–52 who were queried about their language problems in the study just referred to, 30 percent reported no difficulties with English because they came from English-speaking countries. Sixteen percent reported no difficulties despite the fact that they came from non-English-

[2] *Ibid.*, p. 19.
[3] *Ibid.*, p. 19.

speaking countries. Fifty-one percent on the other hand reported some difficulty with language. The majority found the difficulty to lie in understanding other people (47 percent), while a considerable number found difficulty in speaking (25 percent).[4] There is no indication in the report of the duration of these difficulties although this is an essential element in the situation.

Full command of English or any language requires the acquisition of a complex set of auditory and vocal skills as well as the comprehension of a vast range of meanings. Linguists can describe some of these complexities in the technical language of their discipline, but the nonspecialized person knows on an experiential level that there is a vast difference between having a reading knowledge of a language and the ear trained to hear the spoken language. He knows that a competent school level of comprehension is different from even a moderately competent ability to communicate in the language. And lastly he knows that every language is rich in hidden cues of intonation and subtleties of meaning. The degree of command of English which a foreign student brings with him and acquires during his sojourn is indubitably one of his most significant skills, and at the same time a symptom of his capacity to understand and to deal with the American environment, particularly the highly verbalizing environment of colleges and universities. A low ability in aural, oral, reading, or writing English is a serious handicap. All the reports on foreign students from colleges and universities participating in the Carnegie Endowment's program on universities and world affairs attest the practical importance of this fact. It may serve to isolate the student from supportive American contacts on both personal and academic levels. It greatly increases the educational strain, and may reduce the chances of goal achievements that are so essential to satisfactory adjustment. For, in a large degree, the labor required by a student to perform adequately in his studies is a function of

4 *Ibid.*, pp. 15–16.

his mastery of the language. In the case of students who are mature, who are concerned with sciences or laboratory techniques that do not primarily depend upon English, and who have no strong personal needs to relate themselves to a wide social environment, the command of English is not so urgent as for a student of sociology who is gregarious and anxious to "feel the pulse" of our national life.

The practical implications of the foregoing are clear. All students do not need to have a uniformly high level of oral or aural English competence for admission to all schools or courses of study. Language competence is important but it is a function of goals, fields of study, and intended length of stay. Language competence must be judged on an individual basis, and probably any categorical over-all regulation to which selection committees or entrance committees would be forced to adhere would be frequently inappropriate. It does indicate, however, that both in selection and in academic counseling the command of English must be tested and considered in terms of the context of the whole situation.

One additional aspect of command of English sometimes escapes attention: fluency and verbal speed can easily be mistaken for competence. Indian and African students, for example, may long have used English as a secondary or even primary language. The inclination may be to assume that no language barrier exists whereas in fact a whole aural and contextual readjustment may be necessary. This readjustment usually takes place quite rapidly during the spectator phase, but its importance in the first weeks or months of an individual's stay in this country should not be underestimated. Nor should one ignore the possible initial dismay of individuals who, because of their speaking or reading fluency, have assumed an oral or aural competence that they, in fact, do not have. These are usually only transitory initial difficulties but, for reasons discussed elsewhere, the initial difficulties are precisely those to which careful attention should be paid.

Another point is that the acquisition of fluent English may be important social capital in the home country. English as a world language not only attracts students to the United States but once mastered may prove a life asset that in itself justifies a year's study here for some students. Whether educational institutions perceive this as an adequate goal for foreign students is another issue.

A recent survey of the thirty-six institutions in the Association of Graduate Schools revealed that twenty-one of the thirty-four reporting institutions

give no English examination to foreign students, either upon or before entrance to the Graduate School. Nine give such examinations to all entering foreign students, and four give them only to students referred by the departments or by advisers as showing deficiency in the language.

The report of the survey indicates that

the degree of competence in English, as indicated by the examinations, determines whether a student will be required to take special work in English. In eleven schools (of the thirty-four reporting), English courses for foreign students are offered in the English Department; in four, full-time work is offered in a special program; in six, courses are offered in departments other than English, such as Speech or Linguistics; in five, help is provided through individual aid or tutoring; one school sends students to a nearby college. From these data, it is clear that about one-half of the members of the Association of Graduate Schools regard the English ability of students as a problem requiring attention. The University of North Carolina, the Massachusetts Institute of Technology, and Princeton, however, reported very little trouble in this regard because of care in the selection of students.[5]

[5] Association of Graduate Schools, "Journal of Proceedings and Addresses of the Fifty-fourth Annual Conference of the Association of American Universities and Fifth Annual Conference of the Association of Graduate Schools," held in New York City, October 26, 27, 28, 1953, pp. 95–110. Appendix F reproduces in full the statement on language problems in this report (Mimeographed).

The report then suggests the desirability of objective tests for English proficiency and deplores the present highly variable and often unsatisfactory subjective appraisals of a foreign student's English. Although there may be much virtue in ascertaining a foreign applicant's facility in English for the reasons given above, a poor performance should probably not be used automatically to debar a student. Rigidity as well as laxity can have drawbacks. One of the hazards to the success of foreign student programs is the impulse to standardize the English language requirement.

Probably the most constructive solution to all these varied considerations is the administration of a low minimum test of English competence. When minimum competence is revealed, the student should be advised that his sojourn may have to be extended or his educational goals revised. Furthermore, in such cases, strong consideration should be given to placing the student in an institution that provides competent teaching of English as a foreign language. Lastly, it may be wise to bear in mind that undergraduate work often taxes English facility more than many fields of graduate work, although it may be assumed that more graduate than undergraduate applicants possess an adequate command of the language.

Age and Academic Status

Opinions differ markedly on the age and educational status considered appropriate to study abroad. The age of a foreign student is generally assumed to be an important factor in his adjustment. Opinions diverge sharply on whether younger (undergraduate) or older (graduate) students derive more benefits from a study sojourn in the United States. Actually, in 1952–53, 42 percent of the foreign students in the United States were between twenty and twenty-five. Thirty-three percent were over twenty-six.[6] In 1951–52, 38.8 percent of the foreign students were of graduate and research standing.[7]

Educators and foreign student advisers usually favor graduate rather than undergraduate foreign students. The points raised in favor of graduate students range from concern about alienation to questions of administrative convenience. For example, (1) graduate students are usually more mature and therefore develop a better grasp of the host country in a short time; (2) the grasp they develop is more likely to be objective; (3) their shorter stay is less costly to their sponsors; (4) they are more likely to adapt to American culture than to emulate it; (5) they are better able to give Americans an informed picture of their own country; (6) they are less of a counseling problem on the campuses; (7) they have firmer ties in their own countries and are therefore less subject to alienation; (8) they are academically more highly instructed and better selected; (9) they are less likely to present administrative problems; (10) they are more likely to be useful to their own countries upon their return; (11) they have more clearly defined career and study goals and are therefore more likely to concentrate steadfastly on their objectives.

On the other hand, in certain countries whose educational systems are still undeveloped, the number of students at the graduate level may not be sufficient to meet national training needs. Therefore, undergraduates have to be sent abroad. Moreover, if the program's objective is to influence students in favor of the United States, undergraduates may be more impressionable, but the risk is then run of alienating them from their homelands. Particular care must be exercised on this score with undergraduates, although denationalization is a risk that may occur with any age and any academic status.

[6] Institute of International Education, *Education for One World, 1952–53* (New York: The Institute, 1954), p. 11.

[7] Institute of International Education, *Education for One World, 1951–52* (New York: The Institute, 1952), p. 23.

It seems likely that age, *per se,* is less significant than the position of the individual in his educational career. A recent investigation of Swedish returned students [8] indicated that the propitious time for Swedish students to study in the United States is either immediately after taking their *student examen* and before entering a Swedish university, or after completing university work. In the former instance, a United States sojourn of a year may improve the command of English and give the student a general broadening experience. Further, the rigorous discipline of the *gymnasium* at home makes the directed American college system more acceptable. If a Swedish student comes to the American educational scene from the freedom and atmosphere of intellectual maturity encouraged in Swedish universities, he is likely to feel that he has taken a retrograde step and that he is being treated in a puerile fashion. The graduate of a Swedish university, however, who comes for postgraduate specialization may be able to work in the United States in an atmosphere of self-reliance and concentration appropriate to goals that he finds more congenial.

Somewhat similar conclusions were reached in a recent study of returned Japanese students [9] although the reasons were somewhat different.

A Japanese establishes some of his most important associations in higher school and college, both with his peer group and with a clique having power in the field which he is interested in entering. If he fails to establish these relations, because he has studied abroad or has been away from Japan too long, he will have great difficulty in establishing himself on his return. If he goes after these relations are well established, then his foreign experiences are regarded as a

[8] This study was carried out by Dr. Franklin Scott in 1952–53 as one of the research projects supported by the Social Science Research Council's Committee on Cross-Cultural Education.

[9] This study was carried out by Mr. Herbert Passin in 1952–53 as one of the research projects supported by the Social Science Research Council's Committee on Cross-Cultural Education. The quotation cited here is drawn from an unpublished report of the Social Science Research Council's Committee on Cross-Cultural Education (Ithaca Conference, August 1953).

"plus" to his career, one which adds luster to his reputation and polish to his technical abilities. The difference in the return careers of these two groups is so striking that they have to be studied separately. It is often felt that those who take undergraduate work abroad are incapable of making the grade in Japanese society.

In general, then, the student's position in the course of his educational or professional career in the home country rather than his age will determine when he can profit most from study abroad. In those countries that have established university systems geared to produce students who will undertake careers in their country, it appears that study abroad should be limited to a brief one-year sojourn prior to entering the university, or foreign study should be delayed until the university career is completed and the individual's career is assured. In countries in which the higher educational system has not yet been established or is not geared to the career lines of the nation, such considerations may not obtain. In even more general terms it might be argued that an individual should not study abroad during the critical period of role formation, whatever the period happens to be in his particular society.[10]

Duration of Sojourn

The duration of a study sojourn is a related question that is often raised and divergently debated. Like age, its influence is probably highly variable and does not constitute a factor on which over-all judgments can be reached. The desirable duration of sojourn is dependent upon the type and length of training needed to achieve the student's educational goal, his primary group relations, his life chances, and his expectations upon return. For example, a recent study of returned Japanese students suggests that "length of residence in the United States seemed to be an important differentiating factor. The longer

[10] The writer is indebted to Dr. John Gardner for this extension of the original idea.

the residence in the United States, the more balanced was the attitude toward this country; the shorter the stay, the more serious were adjustment difficulties here." [11] If, however, the sojourn is prolonged to the point where contacts are lost with the home country, serious readjustment difficulties may arise.

Another study of some 200 Norwegian Fulbright returnees indicates "very generally, adjustment seems to have been good among those who stayed in America less than six months, adjustment appears also to have been good among those who stayed there more than eighteen months, while those who left America after a stay from six to eighteen months seem to have been less well adjusted. . . ." The U-shaped relationship between duration and adjustment proved in this study to be the effect of a "genuine time process" and "not an effect of time selection of persons differently adjusted." [12]

For administrative purposes, regulations limiting the educational sojourn may be necessary, but if rigidly and broadly enforced either because of financial stringencies, legal requirements, or administrative ineptitudes, such regulations can work at cross-purposes to the best interests of all concerned.

Alienation

Throughout the foregoing pages in which the question of educational status, age, and duration of sojourn have been touched upon, there has run consistently the theme of "denationalization" or "alienation" of foreign students. It may be useful to summarize the suggestions presently available on this score in a series of hypothetical propositions.

Alienation is a function of age, length of sojourn, and the

[11] See Passin study referred to in footnote 9, p. 87.

[12] Sverre Lysgaard, "Adjustment in a Foreign Society: Norwegian Fulbright Grantees Visiting the United States," preliminary draft of a paper prepared for a symposium on Personal Contact and Change in Intergroup Attitudes, International Congress of Psychology, Montreal, June 7–12, 1954 (Mimeographed), pp. 7–8.

nature of the student's stake in his homeland. The younger the student, the longer his stay abroad, and the looser his ties to his country, the greater are the risks of alienation. These risks will be reduced if the student's racial and cultural backgrounds are not readily assimilable in the American scene. Contrariwise, alienation is less likely to occur if the individual's career trajectory at home is clear and promises upward mobility. If life chances at home are circumscribed or even unfavorable, alienation may have set in even prior to departure. To the degree that home ties are closely maintained during foreign residence by association with congenial fellow-nationals, by communications with his family, and by a constructive educational emphasis on readaptation to his own country, the risks of alienation will be reduced.

The knotty question remains that of identifying in an individual the stage at which constructive adjustment may begin to shade over into alienation. There is probably no formula, although one foreign student adviser has suggested that the desire to marry a national of the host country is symptomatic of adjustment to the point where alienation threatens.

Although assimilation to this country and alienation from the homeland are generally presumed to be undesirable, there will nevertheless be cases in which alienation, if not assimilation, is unavoidable. This situation then places a moral responsibility on the individuals who have counseled or befriended him. On this score, many Americans feel that, once the decision to remain in this country is irrevocable, every effort should be made to assist him in that resolve. Others feel equally fervently that students are obligated to return to their home country.

Freedom of Choice

Returning now to a theme which has run consistently through the discussion so far, it appears that self-esteem may be seriously affected, negatively or positively, by the opportunities upon arrival for freedom of choice in such matters as place of study, courses, type of residence, and the like.

Both systematic investigation and experience indicate that freedom of choice upon arrival in the United States can exercise considerable influence on the adaptive phase and perhaps on the whole adjustment process. Even students who come from family or cultural backgrounds at an age when freedom of choice at home is limited seem to expect certain gratifications in this realm from their American experience. Limitations upon such freedoms almost invariably produce more or less obvious and externalized difficulties. These are manifest most frequently in three spheres: the place of study, the subjects studied, and the length of the sojourn. For example, a Syrian student may have expected to study social relations at Harvard, but a scrutiny of his formal qualifications suggests a different institution. Or, an Argentinian wants a Ph.D. in physics, but his scholarship award permits him to stay in the United States only one of the three years required to achieve his goal. Or, several Turkish teachers have hoped to share common quarters in a Southern town during their study period in the United States only to find themselves assigned to dormitory facilities. These are examples so commonplace that even to raise them seems superfluous. But the significant point in relation to all these educational and administrative decisions, many of which may be unavoidable or are in the long run wise, is that they may add to the sense of constriction and frustration in the early phases of the sojourn. The constructive course is, therefore, to facilitate the exercise of informed choice on the part of a foreign student. Where this is not possible or where errors of choice have been made, it is important to provide him with careful explanation and counseling. Thus, administrative convenience or efficiency may have to be sacrificed to the sense of freedom individuals derive from their first experiences with the American scene.

Knowledge of the United States

In chapter 5, "Salient Factors in Prearrival Attitudes," the importance of various elements in a foreign student's background was stressed. Omitted at that stage was specific reference to the knowledge of the United States which a student brings with him. The stock of information as well as the attitudinal set with which a person approaches any new situation can be an important factor in the character of his subsequent perceptions, experiences, and judgments. Foreign students coming to the United States show a tremendous range in this respect. At one extreme are objective, well-informed individuals who may have read more widely and soundly on aspects of American life than have most Americans. At the other extreme are those who arrive with little more equipment than that acquired from American movies and a home press that has not necessarily been either full or impartial in its reporting on American affairs.

On whatever level of sophistication about cross-cultural differences or social analysis a person operates, he can bring no more than his past experience to bear on new situations. It is probable that the actual substantive knowledge of the United States is less important than the emotional set. The usual stereotypes that individuals possess about another country are less important and certainly more transient than the intellectual and emotional habit of thinking stereotypically and of searching for quick, tight formulae.

In counseling foreign students, it may be wise to remember that their substantive knowledge may have less importance than their capacity for suspending judgments and seeking objective answers. There may have been an overemphasis in certain research and evaluation studies on the stereotypes of, and attitudes toward, the United States and insufficient attention to both the flexibility and stability of habitual modes of thought of particular individuals. The study of stereotypes of the United

States in different countries may be useful for determining directions in propaganda policy, but the stereotypes held are less relevant in appraising the learning potential of foreign students. Therefore, in considering the adjustmental potentials of foreign students on arrival, information may have some value but attitudes seem even more significant.

Interpersonal Relations

We have considered so far a series of factors that appear to bear on the constructive adjustment of foreign students, language competence, age and educational status, the intended duration of the sojourn, freedom of choice, and knowledge of the United States. The most important factor was only alluded to earlier in this chapter, namely, the opportunity and the capacity of the individual student to establish warm, supportive interpersonal relations (see also page 41).

In general, a legitimate argument is that interpersonal relations have greater influence on adjustment to a foreign culture than do accidental experiences, administrative regulations, or the material environment. This latter point is not always apparent to Americans who, compared to many other peoples, place a disproportionate emphasis on material well-being. The point to be made is that difficulties with material concerns like housing, food, clothing, and finances can easily and often more appropriately be mediated by supportive interpersonal relations. Attempts of administrators and counselors to deal only with administrative or material difficulties may in many instances result in treating the symptoms rather than the disease.

The patterns of interpersonal relations can be assumed to influence basically the nature and direction of the satisfactions or deprivations an individual feels when he is transplanted not merely among strangers but also among strangers whose patterns of relationship may be different from his own. An individual, for example, whose emotional security has been vested in a mutually supportive joint family can be expected to undergo considerable emotional disorientation when transplanted into an International House. Or, a man who has relied upon a wife and children for emotional support and equilibrium will not find it easy to adjust to the celibate life of a dormitory. The individuals he comes to know intimately may help him more than any other one resource in adjusting to the new situation and in interpreting its significance objectively. Nevertheless, a society that prizes friendship expressed in terms of long, intimate, and self-revealing confidences will ill-prepare an individual for the casual, superficial and extroverted types of friendship so often found in American college life (see pages 62–63).

This may be the appropriate place to discuss the sexual accessibility of members of the opposite sex in the host country. Certainly the tradition of "dating" in the United States can easily be misleading to many foreign students and in certain foreign nationals may entail damage to their self-esteem. For example, Mexican students who frequently arrive believing that American girls are "easy to make" are astonished when this proves not to be the case. The casual, almost impersonal affection often shown by American girls on "dates" may make the Mexican youth feel personally rejected and be construed as an insult to his manhood.

On the other hand, the liberal, premarital sex relations in Scandinavia may make American dating seem both provocative and at the same time "indecently prudish." The Scandinavian male does not seem to suffer in self-esteem but does experience unexpected frustrations in these respects.

The importance of interpersonal relations is underlined in an interesting study of a small group of German students at the University of Michigan. The author suggests that during what has here been called "the adaptive phase," the subjects were seeking assurances that they were liked and respected not only

as representatives of their country but as individuals.[13]   She
states:

If he has numerous opportunities for testing the reactions of
Americans, and if, in this testing, he receives the kinds of assurance
that he wants, this period of testing-out may be shortened. If, on
the other hand, the opportunities for interaction are few, or if they
provide unwanted and unfavorable information, and particularly if
they provide ambiguous and contradictory information, then the
anxieties and resistances of visitors may build up to the point where
it is impossible for any positive learning to take place.

Dr. Watson's point on the importance of consistency in the
information received may perhaps be linked psychologically to
the well-established principle of repetition in learning theory.

Dr. Watson then continues with the following comments on
the subsequent adjustment of the subjects studied.

However, once this period is successfully completed, there are
several important and lasting results. For one thing, there is an
advance in good will—not so much that he likes America better, but
rather, that he is more sure that Americans like him. Secondly, there
is a relaxation of defensiveness about Germany. Finally, there
develops a readiness to learn from America—not to copy . . . but
to observe independently. . . .

Reference Groups[14]

Another point deserves mention in connection with this subject although it lies perhaps half-way between this discussion of
interpersonal relations and the following paragraphs on secondary
group status and role.

The fact is commonly recognized that tourists of whatever

[13] Jeanne Watson, "A Follow-up Study of Cross-Cultural Contact." This
paper was accessible to the author only in mimeographed form. It was
read at the joint meeting of the Ohio Valley Sociological Society and the
Midwest Group of the Society for Applied Anthropology in East Lansing,
Mich., in April 1952.
[14] Reference groups are defined as "those groups to which the individual
relates himself or to which he aspires to relate himself as a part psychologically." Musafer Sherif and M. O. Wilson (eds.), *Group Relations at
the Crossroads* (New York: Harper & Bros., 1953), p. 20.

nationality frequently behave with less restraint abroad than at home. The release from the strictures of one's reference groups facilitates such behavior. Undoubtedly, foreign students may experience to some extent the same release from reference group strictures. If these have been onerous to the individual, the release may be experienced as liberating. But if some new reference group is not established, the release in certain cases may result in the type of irresponsible behavior so often observed in tourists. The degree to which the loss of reference groups may be disorienting, in whatever fashion, is probably a function of the degree to which the individual is "other-directed." [15] Persons who have not internalized their values and who are accustomed to rely upon the views of their peer groups or of authority for their views, for their behavioral standards and their judgments, are undoubtedly more easily disoriented by this loss than are "inner-directed" individuals. However, the other-directed personalities will undoubtedly prove more adaptive to new reference groups than will the inner-directed.

But whether an individual is predominantly inner- or other-directed, his capacity to adjust constructively to even adverse situational, administrative, or material experiences will be mediated by the kind of interpersonal contacts he establishes.

Status and Self-Esteem

This brings us to another point, the social status and the attendant role a foreign student possesses on arrival and the status and roles to which he must adapt in the United States. It was indicated earlier that egalitarianism is a well-developed strand in the fabric of American value systems.

The reluctance of many Americans to recognize such class

---

[15] This term is derived from David Riesman, *The Lonely Crowd: A Study of Changing American Character* (New Haven: Yale University Press, 1950). The author is indebted to Dr. Ithiel de Sola Poole for some of the suggestions contained in this paragraph.

distinction as this country possesses, and the tendency here for the great majority of the people to identify themselves as middle class, have already been implied. In nations where class distinctions have sharper boundaries and more overt recognition, there may also be associated with them certain status expectations and certain roles that are not generally recognized in the United States and, even if recognized, are not easily accepted. Strangers here may be treated with less deference than their social position at home has accustomed them to receive. For example, government-sponsored fellows, either by family position at home or by the very fact that they have received a governmental award, may see themselves quite accurately in their terms as persons of considerable status and importance. If they arrive unheralded in this country, or are met by a person without tact, or find themselves herded through situations as a unit on a par with perhaps dozens of others, there may be, and often is, a sense of pique and a sense of social ineptness on the part of Americans that produces a negative first reaction.

Financial questions may also have important symbolic, as well as practical, implications for foreign students. Dollars the world over are considered a valuable currency. New arrivals often have to learn through hard experience that in the United States the purchasing power of the dollar may be no greater than of the currency at home and may in fact be even less. Students who come from countries where hospitality imposes strong reciprocal obligations may find it difficult to respond to invitations that they would otherwise wish to accept. A reduced standard of living may add to the student's feeling that his status has been impugned, his importance minimized, and his opportunities reduced by transplantation to this country.

Thus when a student comes from a country where wide spans exist in standards of living as well as in distances between social classes (for example, some Near Eastern and Latin-American countries), he is likely to belong to an economically and socially privileged group and to have no experience with the "modest" living standards considered normal for United States students. He may find himself without the dollars for altering this situation and may find social pressures on the campus organized against a disproportionately high standard of living. The young "aristocrat" is distressed not only by being leveled downward but also by his incompetence in coping with gentlemanly amenities of life. On the other hand, a student from a country with an equally aristocratic tradition but where the contrasts in standards of living and social distances are not so great (for example, some West African and European countries) may be able to accept with good grace the modest living standards of American campus life, but he may feel thwarted in his desire to acquire books, equipment, or even "gadgets" he deems necessary or desirable.

The contrary type of situation appears frequently to be the experience of female students from countries that do not grant women a status comparable to that granted them in the United States. Not infrequently such a woman will make every effort, including marriage to an American, to remain in this country. If return is unavoidable, she may find severe difficulties in readjustment.

Thus, similarities between the home and host country with respect to accorded statuses—class differences, standards of living, and the like—ease the process of adjustment. Elaborating this theme, where conditions in the host country compare favorably with those at home, the host country is also perceived favorably. But, if the conditions in the host country compare unfavorably to accepted and expected conditions at home, the perceptions of the host country will be unfavorable.

Such favorable or unfavorable perceptions can be altered, or adjusted to, with no basic trauma to self-esteem so long as supportive interpersonal relations are established to mediate the experience.

Summary

Much of what has been said in the foregoing chapter can now be summarized and somewhat rephrased in terms of the enhancement and diminishment of self-esteem that was discussed earlier (chapter 5, pages 39–41). Whatever equipment the individual brings with him to this country in terms of self-esteem, situations that he encounters here will have varying importance to his adjustment. Among the factors that can be damaging to self-esteem are: inadequate opportunities or abilities to communicate whether because of faulty English, racial barriers, or cultural distance; unfavorable accorded national status (see chapter 5, pages 41–44 for further development of this theme); inability to achieve the expected educational goal whether because of language disabilities, past educational handicaps, poor placement, or restricted freedom of choice; inconsistency of experiences with regulations, study experiences, and personal relations in this country; and, to a lesser degree and more rarely, financial stringencies.

Although these factors do not operate with equal force on all individuals, it seems likely that when several of them operate simultaneously, the greatest damage is done to self-esteem and therefore to a constructive adjustment. In many cases additional time may facilitate adjustment. For example, initial handicaps due to faulty English or to inadequate educational preparation can often be overcome, given enough time. But whatever adjustive difficulties may be encountered, the ability and opportunity to establish one of a variety of supportive interpersonal relationships can go far in mediating situational factors that are potentially damaging to self-esteem.

A wise adviser will provide assistance through psychological counseling and also will try whenever possible to adjust damaging situational factors. To allow for leeway in these respects, administrative regulations governing foreign student affairs, whether those of the Federal Government or of the local institutions, should be minimal and flexible.

Chapter 9

FACTORS
IN POSTRETURN
ADJUSTMENT

THE QUALITY of the sojourn experiences abroad undoubtedly affect a foreign student's postreturn adjustment.[1] Some factors in addition to those already discussed deserve further elaboration. Before discussing them in detail, however, it may be desirable to recapitulate a few closely interlocking points previously suggested that are significant determinants in postreturn adjustment.

First, if the foreign student's decision to study abroad has been dominated by escape motives, he can be expected to have difficulties in readjusting to his own country. For example, certain German and Austrian students in recent years have been discouraged by the future they foresaw for themselves in their home country. They have utilized fellowship opportunities as a preliminary step in hoped-for emigration. Foreign study experiences may only intensify a desire to live abroad permanently.

Second, and closely allied to the first point, if the sojourn

[1] An excellent study has appeared on the postreturn problems of Indian students. See John Useem and Ruth Hill Useem, *The Western Educated Man in India: A Study of His Social Roles and Influences* (New York: Dryden Press, 1955).

abroad is a liberating and generally satisfying experience compared to the home situation, return may present serious difficulties. An example, mentioned earlier, is that of women who come from countries where their status is less gratifying than that accorded them in the United States.

Third, a foreign student will be reluctant to return home if the sojourn abroad is prolonged to the point at which the student's significant personal relations and expectations have a host country setting. Reference has been made to the "firmness of anchorage" that the individual possesses in his homeland. Undoubtedly, firm personal and/or symbolic bonds to the homeland may to some degree offset any reluctance to leave the satisfying experience offered by a foreign sojourn. Contrasts in culture, language, and race also enhance "firmness of anchorage." If the channels to the home country are kept open through frequent and full correspondence, through world news channels, and through consistent and intelligent interest in the home country on the part of hosts, the "firmness of anchorage" will be more durable than if the individual's channels back to the home country are blocked off. In academic language, this raises the interesting and important question of the coexistent activity of past and present reference groups.[2] Obviously, the optimal sojourn period will not be the same for all students; therefore, arbitrary rules about the length of sojourn are inappropriate. In the case of a German youth who has lost his family during the war and sees no hope for himself at home, this factor may be operative even before arrival, whereas an Indonesian youth who has a large family to whom he is deeply loyal and who sees a useful and growing career ahead of him in his home country may easily spend four to six years abroad without losing his desire to return home.

These three points belong to a universe defined in terms of

[2] The writer is indebted to Dr. Charles Loomis for this phrasing of the problem.

individual emotions. However, they can also be viewed externally as part of the larger social framework of life expectations and life chances.

Life Expectations and Life Chances

The importance of the relationship between personal expectations and actualities in the postreturn period was well demonstrated in a study of some thirty returned German leaders. Lippitt and Watson report, for example, that "83 percent of them discovered upon return that their expectations and aspirations exceeded the realities of the back-home situation, and that a third of these made definite plans to leave their own country."[3]

Quite apart from personally projected expectations, a student's life chances upon return may depend upon a series of forces that operate at a national level and that are well beyond his control. Some of these he may foresee while he is still abroad and they may contribute to his reluctance to leave the host country; others may become apparent to him after his return.

As mentioned earlier, relative national stability and national change are major factors in any objective appraisal of life chances. Thus, if a country progresses rapidly in its economic, social, and technical development so that the educated elite can see its career trajectory as a rising one, the returned student may view his home situation positively. However, if employment opportunities for even a needed educated group prove limited at home, or if the educated group is produced at a rate greater than the national capacity to absorb them, serious personal, as well as social and political, repercussions can be expected.

This very obvious proposition makes all the more astonishing the widespread disregard of these factors in national planning

[3] Ronald Lippitt and Jeanne Watson, "Being Strangers—and Returning Home," Background Paper for Group C-2, "Effectiveness of the Interchange of Persons," Fourth National Conference of the U.S. National Commission for UNESCO, September 1953 (Mimeographed), p. 7.

and in the various fellowship programs made available through public and private financing.

One of the few studies of this type deals with Syria.[4] In this pilot study the manpower needs of Syrian developmental plans were compared to the country's educational product. From the comparison were extrapolated the number of Syrians, including their field of specialization, who should study abroad during the next ten years if the nation's developing services were to be competently staffed. For the most part this type of systematic long-range study has been neglected or even ignored. Although such plans cannot, and should not, include all Syrians who would have cross-cultural education, it is nevertheless a constructive approach to the question of life chances for returning students.

Recognition of Educational Experience

On an educational level, a returned student's life chances may be affected by the prestige accorded the educational system of the host country. His chances may also be affected by whether or not his learning experience abroad has included general principles as well as specific techniques and data applicable to the home country.

The question of prestige accorded foreign educational systems represents in itself a wide range of factors. For example, the high development and standards of the Japanese university system are considered in Japan the most valuable education any national can obtain. Those who have taken their university training abroad in recent years run the risk of being considered educational "second-stringers" upon return. On the other hand, such disadvantageous comparisons are not likely to be made between home-trained and foreign-trained Indians, although

[4] Herbert H. Williams, *Foreign Study for Syrians: A Guide to a Long Range Program,* Institute of International Education, Research Program, Occasional Paper No. 4, January 1953 (New York: The Institute).

British training in some fields may be considered superior to American. In certain fields, foreign specialization may be esteemed despite the generally higher prestige accorded the home educational system. In Sweden, there is no lack of confidence in the excellence of the nation's universities, but the desirability of postgraduate work abroad in certain fields of medicine and in the social sciences, for example, is generally recognized. In Mexico preliminary inquiries indicate that the urbanized, upwardly mobile, middle class studies in the United States, whereas the traditional landed aristocracy still turns to a European sojourn for foreign experience. A practical factor is that some students come to study in the United States not necessarily because of preference but because it is the country for which fellowships or grants are available.

All of these factors bearing on the relative prestige associated with different educational systems are further reflected in the whole troublesome question of credits for course work and the validation of degrees across national boundaries. The great number and the wide qualitative range of American educational institutions are factors that frequently handicap students returning to their home countries where both government and education officials have abandoned in despair any effort to evaluate the educational significance of a United States study sojourn. In Mexico, for instance, degrees are required for certain government posts, but the validation of a degree from the United States may prove so difficult that some individuals find it easier to repeat certain studies or examinations at home rather than to have their United States degrees validated. Comparable cases have been reported in Japan.

Associated with prestige of foreign study and problems of credits and validation is the question of the relevance of American education for the returned student—a question to which many educators and officials, both here and abroad, have long been alert. Gross irrelevancies occur only rarely today. An agronomist who plans to work with wet rice agriculture in Thailand is not likely to be sent to a dairy school in the northeastern United States. Less obvious are questions of the basic principles in any field and the ability to translate them effectively into different environments. For example, diagnostic principles in medicine are not usually culturally determined. But if the principles taught assume the existence of elaborate ancillary laboratory facilities that are nonexistent in the home country, the doctor trained abroad may experience more frustration than satisfaction upon his return to medical practice at home. Similarly, the research-minded student in natural science or engineering may be frustrated by the lack of technical equipment to which he had become accustomed in the United States. A study of returned Indian students suggests that for this group at least "broad training proves more valuable than highly specialized training" with the exception of persons who go to the West to learn a specific technique.[5]

Fluctuations in diplomatic relationships between nations can more easily affect an individual's life chances than an individual can affect diplomatic relations. The point is obvious and has already been raised. It needs to be underlined again in the context of readjustment problems. The generally reciprocal cordiality between the United States and Great Britain or Scandinavian countries will undoubtedly ease readjustments (already easy) to the home scene. The sensitive nationalism of new countries is less likely to provide the returning student with a political and social climate favorable to pro-American sentiments that the returned student may bring home. Such sentiments may in fact complicate his reorientation. If national sensitivities have been exacerbated by the presence of American nationals in the home country (tourists in Mexico, technicians and visitors

[5] John and Ruth Useem, "How Effective Is Study Abroad: Advance Report of a Pilot Study in India of Persons Returned from Study in the USA and UK," Washington Seminar on International Affairs: Meeting of Jan. 7 and 8, 1954 (Dittoed; not for publication).

to India, or troops in Japan), the student returning from the United States may find it expedient to exercise the greatest caution in evincing American influences.

These fluctuations are well illustrated by the following quotation from Mr. Passin:

The pendulum of preference with regard to foreign schools in Japan has swung back and forth since 1868. Among the prominent leaders of the Meiji Era, very large numbers had been to the United States for study or observation. But as Japan began to look to Europe for models in government, legislation, constitution, the armed forces, the educational system, etc., interest began to shift from American universities to European ones. By World War I, Europe was the preferred place of foreign study. For a brief period after the end of World War I, because of the defeat of Germany, the stock of United States institutions went up, but it soon declined. By this time, two important tendencies had taken shape. First, it was felt that the Japanese educational system itself was superior, at least for Japanese conditions, to any other in the world. Therefore study at a foreign undergraduate institution was regarded as inferior to study in a first-rate Japanese institution (such as the imperial universities). This attitude resulted both from the inherent development of the Japanese educational system itself, and the mounting nationalism of the inter-war years in Japan. Second, European institutions came to be more highly regarded than American, a process which was hastened by the development of Japanese militarism and the political alignment with Germany. Therefore, most overseas students who had a choice preferred to go to Europe rather than the United States for sustained study. At the end of World War II, this attitude has shifted again, and a pro-American-institution reaction is growing in many areas. This is, of course, based not only on a shift in relative evaluation of the United States as against Europe, but on the fact that funds are available for study in the United States, where they are not for Europe; that Europe is still recovering from the war, while the United States does not have such problems; that it is good to learn something from the victors, rather than from the defeated. [6]

Postreturn Affect toward Host Country

The points raised in the preceding pages bear directly on the

[6] Herbert Passin (see footnote on p. 87).

degree of favorable or unfavorable reaction evoked by the host country upon return. Briefly summarized, one might postulate that the image of the host country after return will probably remain favorable or shift in a favorable direction if the returned student finds a public opinion favorable to the host country and if his foreign experience has provided him with capital which has social value in his homeland.

But after return the image of the host country may shift in an unfavorable direction, or appear to shift in that direction, if the returned student finds public opinion hostile to the host country. It may also be unfavorable if his foreign experience, particularly educationally, proves irrelevant or inapplicable.

The preceding discussion contains no indication of the relative importance that one or another factor may exercise in readjustment. Nor has the subject of the effect of the reinforcement of one factor by another been explored. Between the poles of alienation from one's own society and a constructive readjustment to it lies a whole range of individual adaptations: there are people who remain chronically torn and ambivalent as a result of foreign study experiences; there are those who are able to establish relatively satisfactory deviant roles in the home culture; there are those who deny and encyst the foreign experience and in all outward matters appear to readapt quickly to the norms of the home country; there may be those who are able to live constructively within the orbit of two cultures and derive from them expanded horizons and goals; and there are those in whom study abroad leads to identification with international values and ways of life.

It becomes apparent that the favorable or unfavorable image of the host country that the student retains upon return is closely allied to ease or difficulty of readjustment, especially as manifested in life chances. This places in proper perspective the impact of the sojourn period itself. It is not to be expected that the attitudes acquired during the sojourn will remain fixed and unalterable. Just as foreign students have undergone the profoundly important formative influences of childhood and youth in their own country before they came to the United States, so the great majority will continue to be shaped by their native environment after their return. And even while they are in the United States, their life expectancies and chances (both here and at home) will continue to operate and affect their relationships here. From the viewpoint of a foreign student there has been a long past of conditioning and there will be a long future at home. The sojourn in the United States and the adaptation made to it must be viewed from this perspective.

To conclude, the factors that affect the adjustment of students upon return to their homeland need to be given greater precision through further study. It seems probable, however, that the relation of a student's life expectations in respect to his life chances is one important element in the situation and that his life chances at home will to some degree be affected not only by social changes within his home country but also by the recognition granted in his own country of the educational experience he has had abroad. Official relations and national stereotypes prevailing between the two countries will also be involved. The image of the host country that a student entertains after his return home will not be fixed but will alter with circumstances in the home situation.

The American, however, who is concerned with sojourn adjustment, or perhaps with only a brief period or a small aspect of it, is tempted to place disproportionate emphasis on his own efforts and good intentions. The goals he himself has set for a foreign student may be unrealistically ambitious or even inappropriate. If the American counselor or other interested person reacts within the framework of those American configurations discussed earlier, failure to achieve his goal may incline him to redouble his efforts when, in fact, he should stop to think, to set more realistic goals, and in many cases to reduce his efforts or to alter their direction. For example, if a foreign student does not enter into the social and group activities available at an orientation center, the wise procedure may not be to urge or cajole him but to recognize that perhaps the student is setting for himself a more constructive pace and direction for relating himself to persons and situations in the new environment than did the American program planners. Here again the sociocentrism of American life, the high value we attach to individuals but not to individualism, may prove in certain instances not entirely appropriate.

In all relationships, whether between individuals or between nations, there are two sides to the equation. If the equation is to be solved, both sides must be understood. As Department of State personnel are fond of saying, international relations are a two-way street. But it should be a street on which people meet to converse and not one on which they have head-on collisions.

Chapter 10

TYPOLOGIES AND FORECASTS

THE PRECEDING sections have presented a series of sometimes imponderable and always complexly interrelated factors that bear on cross-cultural education, but they are by no means the total array. Categories, typologies, and paradigms constructed from these factors may appear only to make the issues unnecessarily complicated. In fact, however, if such formulations deal with social and psychological processes, they may have certain predictive implications. For example, if the relationship of certain types of learning situations to the acceptance or rejection of new ideas could be established, the implications for predicting how a foreign student is likely to react to a particular educational institution would have practical value as well as theoretic interest. Unfortunately, such formulations are the end product of long and tedious investigations. These have not yet been completed in cross-cultural education or, for that matter, in very many social fields. A few suggestive efforts in this direction will be summarized in this section. But it cannot be sufficiently stressed how tentative, how fragmentary, and how unproved these formulations are. They represent only preliminary efforts in organizing a range of significant factors and findings.[1]

A. Wants, Expectations, and Situations

What an individual wants from a foreign study sojourn may differ from his expectations. His affective responses to the sojourn may be a function of the way in which the actual situation appears to him in terms of these wants and expectations. Systematically considered, eight types emerge from this relationship between wants, expectations, and situations. The examples used to illustrate these types are almost without exception based on actual cases.

Positive responses can be expected if:

Type 1—Wants and expectations are both high and are confirmed by the situation.

EXAMPLE: A young British physicist wants to study with a particular distinguished American physicist. He expects to be placed in a particular laboratory and in fact does study profitably with the professor of his choice for the length of time desired.

Type 2—Wants are high, expectations are low, but the situation exceeds expectation.

EXAMPLE: A German girl wants a fellowship to study in the United States with the hope of marrying an American man but believes that her chances for such a marriage are not good. In fact, she does marry a suitable American.

[1] The following formulations were developed in August 1953, during the course of a ten-day conference of participants in the Social Science Research Council's Committee on Cross-Cultural Education First Research Phase. Participants were: Ralph Beals, John Bennett, Joseph Casagrande, Oluf Davidsen, Cora Du Bois, Norman Humphrey, Iwao Ishino, Richard Lambert, Richard Morris, Herbert Passin, Franklin Scott, William Sewell, M. Brewster Smith.

Type 3—Wants and expectations are both low, but the situation proves rewarding.

EXAMPLE: The son of a middle-class Costa Rican manufacturer accepts a proffered fellowship to study auto-diesel mechanics in the United States. He expects to take over his father's business and realizes that some knowledge of auto-diesel mechanics will be useful to him; but he would have preferred a year of cultural activities in Paris. His father, however, is unwilling to give him this opportunity. He finds that his year in the United States affords him not only competent technical training but unforeseen cultural opportunities and pleasant personal contacts.

Type 4—Wants are low but expectations are high, and the situation confirms expectations.

EXAMPLE: A young Cuban garage worker from an underprivileged background who had never aspired to formal training is offered one year of practical mechanical training in the United States. His expectations are high and are realized.

Neutral or objective responses can be expected if:

Type 5—Wants are high but expectations are low, and the situation coincides with expectations.

EXAMPLE: A patriotic French author realizes that the United States is one of the great contemporary nations and that a knowledge of this country would add to his range of awareness. He is moderately well informed about the United States. He realizes that a year's sojourn here will not add to the perfection of his style but might give him materials for characters or situations in a novel he is planning. He serves in an American university for one year as an exchange professor where he gathers the kind of material he is looking for.

Type 6—Wants are low, expectations are high, but the situation falls short of expectations.

EXAMPLE: The son of a Swedish furniture manufacturer who

looks forward to taking over his father's firm is of the opinion that a study of American business administration might possibly enhance his business effectiveness. Furthermore, it is customary in his group for a young man to have a year or two abroad before settling down. During his sojourn he discovers that American business administration, or the course of study that he followed, has nothing new to teach him.

Apathetic or defeated responses can be expected if:

Type 7—Wants and expectations are both low, and the situation proves unrewarding.

EXAMPLE: An upper middle-class Italian student has failed his university work at home. He is unwilling to study in the United States but his family insists that he come to this country for a year. He entertains a low opinion of this country's educational, social, and cultural life. He attends a Midwestern state university in a rural community. In the course of his sojourn he makes a minimal adaptation in his studies and in his interpersonal relationships.

Negative responses associated with frustration can be expected if:

Type 8—Both wants and expectations are high, but are situationally denied.

EXAMPLE: A South African Negro trained in Christian Mission circles wants eagerly to advance social democracy in his country, and believes that the United States is the country in which most can be learned about social democracy and its practices. Upon arrival he finds himself discriminated against on racial grounds, the level of racial prejudice greater than he anticipated, and the practice of Christian virtues less pervasive than he expected.

Although these formulations have been phrased and illustrated in terms of adjustment to the host country, whatever diagnostic virtues they possess can equally well be applied to a consideration of the individual's readjustment to his homeland.

Obviously, many objections can be raised to formulations of this type. Wants, expectations, and situations can be treated as units only for preliminary purposes, but for both research and practical purposes these terms must be broken down into empirically determinable elements. Wants and expectations operate with respect to many diverse goals and purposes. How does one weigh a series of wants and of expectations to arrive at a satisfaction or an affect quotient? Is it possible to set up a range of intensity with respect to wants and expectations?

Despite these obvious drawbacks, sufficiently experienced and informed individuals concerned with selecting or advising students may find this formulation a useful preliminary guide in thinking about the adjustments possible for a particular foreign student. An interesting experiment would be for such persons to predict the anticipated adjustment and check their predictions against actualities. The experiment, systematically pursued over a few years, would help to sharpen the practitioners' predictions.

B. Self-Esteem, National Status, and Involvement

In the earlier discussion of enhancement or diminishment of self-esteem in the adjustment of foreign students, the role of felt and accorded national status and the mediating element of the individual's involvement in his national status were brought out (see pages 39–48).

The intent now is to explore systematically the possibilities suggested by these formulations. If they are valid, they should permit at least a degree of predictive reliability. Eight types that emerge from combining these factors are listed and possible illustrations are suggested.

Type 1—is characterized by low self-esteem, high accorded national status, and high involvement.

Perhaps many European students who study in the United States rather than at home or in other European countries belong to this group. If they are here on a United States government fellowship and have interrupted their normal homeland university careers to accept a stipend, the chances are even greater that they belong to this group.

A hypothetical case is a Scandinavian student from the lower urban classes or from a rural area. He sees the opportunity of studying in the United States as a privilege that places on him heavy responsibilities to discharge his role creditably as a cultural ambassador and a representative of his country. Conceivably his self-esteem may be enhanced by study in this country where egalitarianism is a prized value and where his class status at home is either undetected or of no concern. He may do very well in his studies. After his return the enhancement of his self-esteem might persist, at least for a time, because of the status accorded him as a result of study abroad. If his home situation is in fact constructive, he may readjust happily, overcome the handicap of breaking into the normal avenue to a career, and become a useful and adjusted person. But if his American career has been self-enhancing while his return situation is not, he may look with longing to this country and wish to return. The seeds of alienation may have been planted.

Type 2—is characterized by low self-esteem, high accorded national status, and low involvement.

Type 2 differs from Type 1 only with respect to the involvement of his self-esteem with national status. An individual who belongs to this type closely resembles Type 1, except that his low involvement in national status will not lead him easily into assuming the role of a cultural ambassador. He may be less sensitive to hostility toward, or ignorance of, his homeland. And his vulnerability in these areas at least will be lower than that of the individual in Type 1. If his experience abroad is self-enhancing, he will interpret it as an appreciation of himself as an individual. If his experience is self-diminishing, he will presumably not develop defenses that are chauvinistic in character although he may develop other kinds of defenses and even break psychologically. One might speculate further and suggest that like Type 1, if the self-enhancing experiences of the United States are found not to be available to him on his return, he may wish to emigrate to the United States. He may be readier to emigrate than Type 1, since his psychic investments in his homeland are presumably more tenuous. He may even foresee before he leaves the United States that the homeland will not offer him the personal advantages of this country, and make every effort to remain here. The seeds of alienation may have found fertile soil.

There are some Americans and a good many north Europeans who would seem to fit this type. Many Americans abroad, for example, hold positions of importance greater than would be accorded them at home and generally enjoy higher status. They make every effort to remain abroad permanently.

Type 3—is characterized by high self-esteem, high accorded national status, and low involvement.

Type 3 differs from Type 2 with respect to his self-esteem. Type 3 has high self-esteem; Type 2 has low self-esteem. This type can be illustrated by the case of an American student. The man is a graduate student who takes a justified pride in his command of French and in his intellectual and philosophic proclivities. He comes from a well-established family in a Middle-western city, has gone to the best schools, served a stint in Korea, but his Army career is not an episode on which he dwells. He has no political interests. In sum, he is as much the young esthete as we are likely to produce in this country. He has just spent fourteen months in Paris. On arrival he avoided tourists and the American colony. He sought out Frenchmen and was eager to take every opportunity to know them. He found the taxi drivers, the waiters, the concierge frequently obsequious but rarely friendly. He bristled a bit in the cafés when French radicals berated him for the latest American policy moves in the European Defense Community and in Indochina. (After all, we are all inclined to be more defensive, more patriotic, perhaps even a little chauvinistic, when our government is criticized to us while we are abroad even though we would make the same criticisms ourselves or would take less umbrage if they were voiced to us by visiting foreigners while we were smugly ensconced at home.) However, he learned rapidly that it is a common failing not to distinguish between national policy and people. Additionally, and perhaps more importantly, he learned that the United States is accorded high status but that hostility in France toward some of our national policies is also high. Since his self-image was not deeply involved in his American nationality, this hostility left him relatively unscathed. The young man's over-all adjustment to France was excellent. He has returned to the United States more mature in his appreciations and judgments about both France and the United States. Thus Type 3 is characterized by high self-esteem, high accorded national status, and low involvement. This is the type of the eight theoretical types that can be expected to be least vulnerable while abroad and that may derive most benefits from such a sojourn. The Social Science Research Council's study of Scandinavian students indicates that many of them may belong to this category, as probably do many other north Europeans who come to the United States to study.

Type 4—is characterized by high self-esteem, high accorded national status, and high involvement.

Individuals of this type are probably not found too frequently among foreign students. Such a person is likely to be so completely and so satisfactorily invested in the homeland—so satisfied with his life chances—that he is not likely to be convinced that a foreign country has much to offer him. If he studies abroad, it usually is with very precise goals in mind. If he encounters adverse opinions of his country while in the United States, he will probably shrug them off with condescension. It seems unlikely that a foreign study sojourn would affect his image of himself or of his country very deeply. At most he might develop certain skills. In speculating about this type, one would expect to find in it people who are not highly tolerant of incompatabilities between national value systems and who do not readily accept the idea of emigration or of prolonged residence abroad. They are more likely to think in terms of a position at home or at most in their own diplomatic corps. They are not likely to possess attitudes that make them good international servants.

Type 5—is characterized by low self-esteem, low accorded national status, and high involvement.

Type 5 individuals may frequently be found among students who come from colonial or recently colonial areas. They are the upwardly mobile young men and women with high aspirations who are deeply dedicated to either the welfare of their people or the recognition of their national state.

The case of a young Nigerian illustrates Type 5. He was born in a village community. He attended a mission school where he picked up not only a reasonably adequate British classical education but also acquired a deep sense of dedication to his people. He wants to become a teacher and he is a nationalist. He failed a competitive examination for a British fellowship which would have taken him to London. This experience served somewhat to dampen his self-esteem but also it seems to have reinforced his nationalism. He settled for an

American fellowship. He knew about race prejudices in the United States, but felt reasonably secure in this respect. At least he had been well briefed and thought he was prepared to deal with this particular barbarism in a strange land. What he was not prepared for was to have a charming hostess say to him at tea upon his arrival in New York, "Oh, Nigeria, how interesting. Tell me, is that in the Pacific or in Southeast Asia?" Nor was he prepared to have an American student who hopes to become an anthropologist say earnestly from behind horn-rimmed spectacles, "Tell me confidentially, Mr. Jones, does your father still practice cannibalism?" Such a student may make little effort to understand and associate with Americans; may not be tempted to remain in this country any longer than is required to finish his education; and may leave the country with no very strong affection for it and probably with many misconceptions.

Type 6—is characterized by high self-esteem, low accorded national status, and high involvement.

Individuals in Type 6 differ from the preceding Type 5 only with respect to their self-esteem. Both are patriotic individuals from countries accorded low status. But individuals in Type 6 are more likely to come from well-established and even aristocratic elites in their homelands, whereas those in Type 5 are more likely to be persons who are upwardly mobile in their native society.

Of the two types, probably Type 5, the individuals with low self-esteem and high involvement, have some chance to experience enhancement of self-esteem in a favorable American situation. Type 6, however, with high self-esteem and high involvement are almost sure to suffer some sense of diminished self-esteem in this country.

In both of these types, one may expect to find individuals who have inflated the image of the United States quite unrealistically before leaving their own country. This inflated image may be charged with either positive or negative affect. In these two types one may also expect to find that once they have arrived in the United States, they will become deeply preoccupied with new ideas about their homelands that are frequently quite defensive in cast. As a result they may be less open to learning and to change than persons who belong to certain other constellations we have been discussing. These are the individuals who may entertain often quite inconsistent and even contradictory ideas of both their home country and the United States. And they may be the individuals most prone to conceal the influence that the United States has had upon them if they meet criticisms on that score at home.

Of the two types, individuals in Type 5 may suffer the greater emotional difficulties but they will express less open hostility during their sojourn than will those in Type 6.

Type 7—is characterized by low self-esteem, low accorded national status, and low involvement.

Like Type 4—high self-esteem, high accorded national status, and high involvement—Type 7, with low self-esteem, low accorded national status, and low involvement, is probably not too frequently found among foreign students in the United States. Possibly certain stateless students belong to this type. Type 7 might also be a child of a low-ranking foreign representative from an underdeveloped country whose parents have moved from one diplomatic or business post to another during most of his life. It might be postulated that he will be characterized by a genuinely passive and docile approach to his education and a ready but shallow adaptiveness to his environment. One can imagine some educators and administrators feeling well disposed toward such a person. But the competent student adviser will find he needs the most experienced and solicitous psychological counseling.

Type 8—is characterized by high self-esteem, low accorded national status, and low involvement.

Like Types 4 and 7, this type is not likely to be represented in large numbers among foreign students in the United States. Such individuals, for example, might be scions of a traditionally entrenched aristocracy in the Near Eastern countries or Latin America. They and their families are not devoted to changing the social order of their homelands. By and large, such individuals are inclined to prefer travel to study and to prefer Europe to the United States. Their attitudes toward the United States will be objective although interlaced with condescending stereotypes about our cultural achievement. They are unlikely, in contrast to Types 5 and 6, to adopt defensive attitudes about their homelands.

This series of suggested types is vulnerable to the same reservations raised about typologies in the section on "Wants, Expectations, and Situations." The types suggested are "ideal" and therefore represent extremes. In actuality, a large number of students cannot be fitted properly into these categories—those whose self-esteem is moderate, who come from countries of middle accorded status and with which they are only moderately involved. There is a further danger in its very manner of presentation. The illustrations and speculations marshaled for each of these types are in the highest degree tentative. Too, there is always the danger that illustrations rather than the types will be recalled by those who read and run. It can only be hoped that this section will be read with caution and will be considered as a point of departure for systematic and careful investigation.

C. National Diagnoses

A very different order of prediction may be based on an intimate knowledge of the sociology and culture of a foreign student's homeland and an equivalent knowledge of the United States. For example, Professor Ralph Beals,[2] who has devoted the larger part of his professional career as an anthropologist to the Mexican scene, feels a high degree of confidence in predicting the adjustments and readjustments of Mexican students who come to the United States, if he knows the particular individual's class and cultural background, and his position and attitudes toward some twelve diagnostic elements such as family background, formal learning, property, money, work, etc. It appears highly probable that this kind of "country specialist" develops certain more or less explicit diagnostic criteria. Whether or not he is professionally trained in psychosocial analysis, he becomes more sensitive to the adaptive processes in nationals of the country he knows well.

This type of diagnostic prediction, however, would entail a systematic study of the seventy or eighty countries that send students to the United States. It would require the kind of formulation upon which few social scientists at the present stage of social science development would be willing to stake their professional reputations. It appears unlikely then that such a systematic guide based on national diagnoses could, or should, be prepared in the immediate future. Furthermore, were such a guide to become publicly available, it would undoubtedly be offensive to national sensitivities in many instances. Lastly, it would undoubtedly run the risk inherent in all such diagnostic tools of being interpreted too crudely so that central tendencies, however correct as such, would be used to stereotype individuals. Although there is much to be said for the national diagnostic approach, its immediate usefulness for individual counseling appears limited.

[2] Professor Beals was director of the Social Science Research Council's Committee on Cross-Cultural Education study of Mexican students in the United States and succeeded the late Professor Wendell Bennett as chairman of the committee.

This judgment, however, is not the equivalent of saying that American campuses should not utilize the faculty members who do have cross-cultural experience in particular countries or areas. The university and college self-surveys conducted at the instigation of the Carnegie Endowment afford evidence that, while many institutions are not utilizing adequately these professional resources, other institutions are using them with excellent results. Nor is this judgment the equivalent of saying that guides cannot be developed on a national basis for the improvement of program administration.

D. Personality Types

The reader may have been struck by the absence of any attempt to deal with foreign student adjustments on the basis of personality types despite the fact that psychological concepts have been freely used. The reason is clear. Psychological typologies are considered even by many of their proponents as scientifically premature and far too ethnocentric. Although psychologists have suggested certain categories that may cut across national boundaries—for instance, the authoritarian versus democratic personality [3]—the relevance for our purposes of such categories is open to question. And if a psychological typology is to be useful at this stage, it must derive directly from data on cross-cultural education. It is unlikely that such a typology can be advanced at present. Nevertheless, an effort in this direction, based on a limited Japanese sample, is suggestive enough in its wider implications to warrant mention here. Dr. John Bennett and his associates have tentatively formulated the following:

The [Japanese] students now coming to the United States seem to fall into two major groups: (1) A "conforming" type, who are generally conservative in their social outlook, who have relatively well established careers in the sciences and technical professions,

[3] T. W. Adorno and others, *The Authoritarian Personality* (New York: Harper & Bros., 1950).

and who are primarily oriented toward improving their knowledge and training; and (2) an "intellectual" type, who are generally liberal in their social outlook, and who often do not have established careers and jobs at home. Or, if they do, they tend to be primarily concerned in their American experience with finding themselves, or finding spiritual values in American life, rather than with their careers as such. The former group, the conformers, tend to see in America what they want, namely, a stable, powerful country, with well-developed techniques for acquiring wealth and status—but at the same time avoiding the annoying status restrictions and pettiness of Japanese society. The intellectuals tend to see America in a different light: as a free, democratic, equalitarian country, where the individual is able to develop his life as he wishes. They join with the conformers in admiring the relative status-freedoms of social interaction of Americans, but differ with them on the issues of power, wealth, class inequality.

As to adjustment, it can be said that on the whole, the conformers seem to make a more congenial adjustment to American college life, and also seem to profit most from their stay. Their professional career goals are satisfied with relative ease, and they seem to have relatively less difficulty than the intellectuals in responding to Americans in social interaction. The intellectuals, on the other hand, find difficulty in making contact with Americans at the deep intellectual level toward which they aspire. And if they are placed in a university which does not have much in the way of philosophical and literary interests, they are likely to experience frustration. Moreover, in the case of the intellectuals, there are powerful trends in Japanese circles toward an oppositional position with respect to American foreign policy, and this often places the foreign student intellectual in a different, ambivalent position.[4]

Elsewhere Dr. Bennett summarizes these two types under different designations when he says, "Foreign visitors with a conservative-accepting social outlook ('conformers') get along better in the United States; but those who are questioning-critical ('intellectuals') understand more about the United States."[5] Dr.

---

[4] "The Adjustment of Japanese Students to American Life," Background Paper for Group C-2, "Effectiveness of the Interchange of Persons," Fourth Annual Conference of the U.S. National Commission for UNESCO, September 1953 (Mimeographed), pp. 5–6.

[5] Manuscript of remarks by John W. Bennett, Attachment C to Ted F. Silvey's memorandum . . . included in report of Fourth Annual Conference of U.S. National Commission for UNESCO, September 1953.

Bennett then goes on to say that:

The two types described above are not the only ones that can be made. Other important differences between outlook and adjustment are found on the basis of educational background, age, family status, and sex. The latter is particularly important: it was found that Japanese women students have a series of distinctive problems which set them off from the men as a group. These problems center upon their search, in America, for a more satisfying expression of their interests and aspirations, as over against the relative restrictions of Japanese female role definition.

In spite of these differences in adjustment patterns, it is found that Japanese students in general tend to withdraw among themselves to an extent greater than that observed for foreign students of all other nationalities. Overtly the Japanese student presents a picture of a rather shy, embarrassed individual, who has difficulty expressing himself (regardless of how good his English may be), and seems to have trouble identifying the precise status of himself *vis-à-vis* others—particularly, Americans. The Japanese student feels that America is a superior nation, and Americans, as people, occupy a generally higher status than Japanese. This makes it difficult for him to respond to Americans with the freedom and friendliness that Americans expect, because free, friendly behavior is not defined, in Japanese socialization, as appropriate for relationships in which statuses are unequal. Individual Japanese students succeed in varying degrees in rationalizing and conquering these ambiguities, but it constitutes a problem for all.

This suggestion of "conformer" and "intellectual" types, based on Japanese data, may have wider applicability. However, such observations do not readily fit any of the various other typologies so far suggested. Presumably, if all formulations are on the right analytic track, it will be possible to synthesize them on the basis of future studies.

E. Types of Learning

Developments in the psychology of learning and perception promise eventually to shed considerable light on the adjustment processes in cross-cultural education. However, there is, at present, only one study known to the writer that has certain specific and relevant bearing on the subject at hand. In 1950 a group of American students under the auspices of the International Relations Clubs spent two months in Europe, one in organized study and one in free travel. Dr. Hilda Taba used factor analyses in an evaluative study of this tour. She evolved a threefold typology [6] in connection with the study. Dr. Taba is the first to realize that such a typology is only tentative and may not represent the full range of variations present in the study group. But at the same time it may prove a helpful guide to future research as well as to immediate interpretations of learning in a foreign scene.

Type 1 had the ability and inclination to internalize new learning into an intellectual and attitudinal framework and . . . this type tended to use specific learning to modify general concepts and feelings, . . . to change . . . viewpoints consciously and systematically. . . .

Types 2 and 3 were different in that their main basis for cultural orientation was strongly emotional and therefore tended to be irrational. In Type 2 this is manifested by their tendency to define one culture by projecting into it either negative or positive characteristics of another, the choice depending on their generalized attitude toward the other. This type of orientation prevented rational and cautious change. Lacking intellectual control over their cultural concepts, experiences with a foreign culture produced illogical shifts and sometimes irrational reversals without a correction in reasoning. . . .

Type 3 was handicapped mainly by a crystallized ethnocentrism. This tended to inhibit full use of new experience, since it introduced selectivity of response to it and imposed on its content an interpretation in terms of the value standards of the home culture.[7]

Types 2 and 3 displayed weakness in their ability to use general principles as an aid in developing perspective, as well as emotional fixations of one sort or another. Because their strong feelings blocked free use of new facts and experiences, they tended to resist change. These fixations also caused a variety of irrational mechanisms to control the formation of cultural orientations. For example, people with a negative attitude toward France, but strong identification with the United States and idealization of its values, tended to project

[6] Hilda Taba, *Cultural Attitudes and International Understanding: An Evaluation of a Study Tour,* Institute of International Education, Research Program, Occasional Paper No. 5, June 1953 (New York: The Institute).

[7] Taba, *ibid.,* pp. 63–64.

on France characteristics that were different from, or opposite to, their concept of the United States. Persons who were positively disposed to France, but had negative or critical attitudes toward the United States, projected the opposite of what they criticized about the United States on France and thus idealized it. The orientation of these individuals was governed, not by an objective system of facts and values, but by their emotional disposition and biases.

These emotional fixations limited learning in several ways. First, they tended to make individuals insensitive to ideas, facts, or experiences that challenged these fixations. They were selective in what they saw, reacted to, or understood. Secondly, when combined with inability to conceptualize or generalize or to use other rational processes of thinking, the impact of new experiences tended to be confined to specifics. Reality corrections were too piecemeal to produce appreciable change in cultural orientation. When these factors were combined with a tendency to stereotype, complete and unwarranted reversals of attitudes took place. The stereotyped mode of thinking was perpetuated while a new attitude was adopted. As a consequence their learning was somewhat unsystematic and capricious. Their attitudes and viewpoints shifted from situation to situation because they either used different criteria for judgment in each case or else their interpretations were arbitrary or accidental.

Finally, it seems that changes in cultural orientation involved in all cases a sequence of steps, the nature of which varied depending on the constellation of the factors with which the individual started. The sequence in attitude formation usually was neither a direct road from favorable to unfavorable views nor the reverse, but consisted instead of a series of corrections toward reality which was accompanied by attitude change in either direction. People with relatively strong stereotypes of the Ideal Society, a critical disposition toward the United States, and an inclination to idealize France (Type 2), were apt to develop a less favorable, but at the same time a more realistic idea of France. However, highly ethnocentric individuals (Type 3) intensified their criticism of France and strengthened their biases in favor of the United States.[8]

At this stage it is not possible to equate Dr. Taba's and Dr. Bennett's types. Nevertheless, there appears some indication that the Japanese "intellectual" type and the American Type 2 have in common the tendency to define a new culture by projecting into it the characteristics felt as positive or negative in another

[8] Taba, *ibid.*, pp. 67–68.

culture and that both are faced with the problem of resolving the resultant ambiguities.

In conclusion, what students want, expect, and actually experience, the degree to which their self-esteem is enhanced or diminished, their national backgrounds, their personality structure, and their learning capacities are all matters that bear significantly on their study sojourn abroad. If future research can establish valid categories, define important relationships, and formulate regularities in adjustment processes, it should be possible not only to select candidates suitable to different programmatic goals but also to provide them with opportunities and experiences relevant to their needs and capacities. Inadequate as are the formulations, they suggest that eventually some degree of prediction about groups of students may be achieved and a higher quality of administrative and educational guidance than in the past may be provided.

Summary of Part Two

In Part Two the emphasis has been placed on foreign students as social-psychological entities rather than on the administrative and programmatic aspects of study abroad. Nevertheless, the implications of social and psychological factors for practitioners in exchange programs have been brought out whenever possible. For each person study abroad is only an episode in a total life experience. Foreign students approach the host country with widely varying wants, expectations, and information about both this country and its educational system. Of importance in an individual's prearrival set is his self-esteem; his involvement with his national status, both felt and accorded; and the firmness of his anchorage in the home scene as mediated, in part, by his life expectations and his life chances at home, by his social status, and by his position in his educational career.

Upon arrival in the United States, he encounters certain American values and institutions that will differ more or less markedly from those in his past experience. Chapter 6 deals with some of the aspects of American life that foreign students repeatedly comment upon and that are therefore assumed to be relevant to their adjustment to the American scene.

In that adjustment four phases were tentatively suggested: the spectator, the adaptive, the "coming to terms," and the predeparture. In keeping with the view that study abroad is only an episode in an individual's life experience, three postreturn phases were also assumed to exist with a final "coming to terms" phase in the homeland that can range from acceptance of national norms to alienation from the homeland. Factors that seem important in such life experiences were discussed: for example, language facility; age and academic status; the duration of the sojourn; freedom of choice; and the quality of interpersonal relations established. It is believed that other elements also operate in the adjustments of foreign students: for example, reference groups, and the relationship of an individual's class status at home to his self-esteem in the United States.

Similarly, factors affecting postreturn adjustments were discussed in chapter 9. Finally in chapter 10 several crude preliminary efforts were made to relate significant factors to each other, thereby providing a series of tentative typologies whose value lies not in categorizing foreign students but in providing those who deal with them in one or another capacity a few clues to understanding them better.

PART THREE

The Relationship of American Colleges and Universities to Foreign Students

WHEN THE Carnegie Endowment for International Peace suggested that a series of volumes be prepared in connection with its program on Universities and World Affairs, it was hoped that they would prove of certain practical value to those concerned with American higher education. In respect to the foreign students in American educational institutions various approaches were possible. A volume might be addressed to American educators from the viewpoint of the public and private administrators of foreign student programs. Certainly there is a recognized need to explain the goals and procedures of these two groups to each other. This is an effort, however, which is perhaps best pursued in conversational exchanges, in conferences, and in the many other personal interactions that are now provided. Public agencies like the Department of State and the Office of Education (with their

131

varied semiautonomous boards and committees), private institutions like the Institute of International Education and the National Association of Foreign Student Advisers, and educational groups like the American Council on Education—to name only a few—are deeply concerned and admirably active in providing opportunities and funds for exchanging among themselves information about common problems of intent and operation.[1]

A volume might also be addressed to American educators on the subject of foreign students from the viewpoint exclusively of American educational institutions. Since American education is far from being monolithic, such a treatment would of necessity be as varied as American colleges and universities themselves. To the extent that each institution of higher education in the United States has some degree of autonomy in framing its objectives and its policies, it has also an independent approach to its foreign students.

A third approach to a volume on the relationship of American colleges and universities to foreign students might be that of foreign students themselves or of the foreign governments that send them here for training. A fourth approach might be that of the local community organizations that have taken a keen interest in foreign guests or immigrants to this country. A fifth approach might be that of the American student not only as he meets and mingles with other nationals in our educational institutions but also as he experiences or contemplates his role as a possible student abroad. In all these approaches it can be assumed that American educators have genuine reason for concern. From all of them practical considerations necessarily spring.

---

[1] Many lists of organizations that are concerned with foreign student programs are available. A brief but carefully selected listing is available in the Institute of International Education's *Handbook on International Study: 1955* (New York: The Institute, 1955).

In this particular and partial discussion of the relationship between foreign students and institutions of higher education in the United States three basic assumptions have by now been amply demonstrated. First, the only indisputable function of study abroad is education. American educational institutions therefore become the most important mediators of this function for foreign students. The second assumption is that an understanding of the wide range of social and psychological factors that are manifest in our foreign student population will assist American educators in formulating policies that are both wise and practical in respect to foreign students but that are at the same time consonant with their own institutional objectives. Third, it has been assumed that in many instances American institutions of higher education must operate within the framework of the broader opportunities and limitations that are provided by noneducational institutions for bringing foreign students to the United States.

In the first part of this volume emphasis was placed primarily on the broad social and administrative implications of foreign student programs. It was phrased largely from the perspective of administrative agencies. Part Two attempted to delineate the elements that make for one or another variety of adjustments to this country on the part of foreign students themselves. It was phrased largely from the perspective of the research worker in social science, but the practical implications for both administrators and educators were stressed whenever possible. In this section emphasis is more particularly placed on the role of educators, educational administrators, and educational advisers as they must deal with foreign students within the framework of institutional administration, community relations, and their primary role as educators of American youth.

The task of educators, if competently and sensitively executed, is complex and frequently baffling. It may involve emotional strain and often entails confusion about the proper position to take in the face of conflicting obligations. There is always at least the temptation to resort prematurely to managerial techniques and to formulate regulations. If these are premature and based on less than full consideration of all pertinent factors they may at best palliate symptoms but may not touch underlying issues. Managerial techniques may often serve the same function as rituals in primitive societies, and when action outstrips understanding, procedures are likely to be made paramount to substance. It has long been recognized that ". . . when human beings are confronted with situations that are beyond empirical control and that are, therefore, anxiety-producing both in terms of emotional involvement and of a sense of cognitive frustration, they respond by developing and elaborating nonempirical ritual that has the function of relieving emotional anxiety and of making some sense of the situation at the cognitive level." [2]

In this situation two levels of anxiety may develop. There is the original or primary anxiety that stems from the desire to accomplish certain results for which there may not be the proper comprehension or techniques to assure attainment of objectives. And there is the secondary anxiety that derives from the nonperformance or improper performance of the managerial procedures. There can be certain hazards in too many and too obsessionally pursued regulations. All who are familiar with questions that arise with respect to foreign students will be able to recall instances in which not only the primary but also the secondary type of anxiety were clearly evinced, usually by the most conscientious individuals.

There is also in the American scene a tendency to specialize and professionalize. The "social engineers," like the medical

---

[2] Evon Z. Vogt, "Water Witching: An Interpretation of a Ritual Pattern in a Rural American Community," *Scientific Monthly*, September 1952, p. 175.

specialists, tend to replace the old-fashioned humanists and the family practitioners. Such new professional groups run the risk of being self-enhancing rather than subject-enhancing. In fact, the subject is likely to be lost sight of in a series of divided responsibilities resulting from specialization. Procedures are likely to take precedence over the ultimate referent—the students from abroad.

In the following section, a series of accepted "managerial" categories are discussed, but an attempt is made to see them from the viewpoint of the education of foreign students rather than from the viewpoint of administrative procedures.

Chapter 11

ARRIVAL ON AMERICAN CAMPUSES

In EARLIER chapters the attempt was made to place programs for cross-cultural education in the perspective of the changing role of the United States in world affairs and to discuss some of the goals and motives that operate in this field. If one sees such programs in the context of the sum total of binational relationships, their ancillary position is clear. The influence of eight hundred German-American study exchangees will not balance the impact of an Army of Occupation. The presence of five hundred French students in the United States and of one thousand American students in France during any one year cannot be equated to the influence of thousands of American tourists in that country each summer or the American government's policy on Indochina. It is necessary, therefore, to assume a modest position about the role of cross-cultural study in the realm of binational relations.

Planning and Continuity

Even if one begins with a modest position, it is possible to enhance or diminish the effectiveness of education abroad by organizational means. The most important of these means is

136

a type of organization that can plan coherently and realistically over a period of at least a decade. If one considers the isolated individual who comes to the United States on his own resources, one may, as an administrator, be cavalier about personal failures or gratified by successes. But if a college or university as an institution admits any concern for foreign students, a different level of responsibility is entailed. It is a responsibility that requires informed programming.

The essential components of any effective program, as contrasted with isolated cross-cultural education, seem to be realistic and precise goals, on the one hand, and continuity on the other. The importance of continuity is particularly evident from still another point of view. As yet, there can be in the execution of educational exchange programs no substitute for experience. The complicated procedures and the judgments they involve are not acquired or transmitted overnight. The personnel concerned with such programs should not only be of high quality but should also be relatively stable in their positions. They should be given time to acquire experience. For example, the rapid turnover of personnel in the United States government agencies or in the Institute of International Education and the haste for evaluative conclusions deemed necessary for Congress or for foundations indicate an incomplete understanding of cross-cultural education as an element in binational relations. It is to be hoped that educational institutions will not duplicate such haste and instability.

These considerations raise serious questions with respect to certain programs. If the practical considerations are such that official or semiofficial programs must be phrased with vague goals, or that they must be given short-term even though definite goals, if they must be carried on a fluctuating budget or one that must be constantly justified—then, these programs begin, and must continue to operate, with serious handicaps. These difficulties have been widely recognized and have led some individuals with high standards to question the validity of all programs so handicapped. They are the individuals who recognize that quality is the essence of worth-while exchange programs and that quantity and discontinuity do not compensate for, but actually may endanger, the good repute in which educational exchanges are generally held in this country. For example, even the diplomatically admirable and well-intended Fulbright program has been criticized.

The objectives of the basic Fulbright program are not clear. They are not spelled out in the basic Act. Insofar as the objectives are stated in other government documents, they appear to be of the generalized cultural-exchange variety, in the hope that exchange of persons will advance international understanding and good will. This lack of precise objective reflects itself at all stages of the operation from selection to follow-up, which are not tied together by force of commonly recognized purpose. Those who would appraise the project must, in large measure, create their own image of objectives to raise as a standard of measurement. . . . Government has a limited capacity for flexible and adaptive experimentation. Private foundations can make a special contribution through creative fulfillment of that function. . . . In our view, a wise policy of exchange should be on a relatively long-term basis. . . . It should concern itself primarily with quality—procedures and grantees—rather than quantity. This should stress a highly individualized and personalized program for each participant. . . . The formulation of clear purposes and objectives will set the basis for improved planning, selection, placement, orientation, content, evaluation, and follow-up. . . .[1]

The foregoing quotation indicates clearly the role that planning and continuity should play in the establishment of any programmatic effort in the field of cross-cultural education. These considerations by no means invalidate conclusions suggested earlier that a multiplicity of programs is desirable in order to have represented a multiplicity of goals. It also does not preclude, but on the contrary supports, the desirability of flexible and personalized programs on the part of administra-

[1] Haverford College, *Report by a Committee of Eight, Fulbright Supplementary Project,* June 8, 1953 (Mimeographed).

tive personnel. Patently there should be no attempt in enabling legislation to spell out specific goals. The need for long-range efforts is also clear. Only in such terms can the "managerial" aspects of programs be appropriately structured and appropriately executed. The educational institutions of the United States have an obligation not only to set a clear and explicit example in this respect but also to assist those who are dealing in public or private programs to give careful thought to consistent long-range planning.

Selection.—For example, from the point of view of achieving goals, selection has been recognized as a subject on which attention should be focused. It is also a subject on which many views exist. The valuable experience of the postwar binational selection committees as well as that of many foundations such as the Scandinavian-American Foundation, the Belgian-American Education Foundation, the British Council, the Rockefeller Foundation—to mention only a few—has unfortunately never been systematically formulated and disseminated. If any one recommendation seems pertinent, it is that just such experience be placed at the disposal of all who are concerned with the vital and crucial question of selection. We need to know not only the American experience and judgments in these matters but also that of other nationalities who have both sent students abroad and received them from abroad.

The Institute of International Education reports that it works at present through 118 selection committees in 74 countries. These are all voluntary committees whose members are prominent businessmen, educators, professional persons, and government servants. The criteria for selection most frequently mentioned are: academic ability, knowledge of English, character and leadership, value of the field of study to the home country, and world understanding. Certainly, some of these criteria reflect programmatic rather than educational goals. How, in fact, such criteria are interpreted within different national contexts or even by differently constituted committees within one nation deserves intensive study. It seems doubtful that world understanding means the same thing to both an Israeli and an Indian. It is even less likely that "character" and "leadership" have the same meaning in Peru and in Burma.

At present, selection procedures are based most frequently on a scrutiny of the applicant's academic records, his letters of recommendation, and an examination in English competence, although the standards in these matters vary greatly from country to country. Selection groups, even the binational commissions of the Fulbright awards, rarely operate systematically to provide personnel needed to fill the development plans of the country. In part, this reflects the absence of integrated thinking and studies that relate programs for foreign study to national planning and the developing need for specialized personnel. It may also reflect considerable ignorance of the goals, standards, procedures, and qualitative variation in American educational institutions. Certainly an important use of federal grants to visiting leaders would be to bring members of foreign selection committees to this country so that thereafter they might operate from a broader base of information about American education.

There is considerable question whether these criteria are equally valid for all countries sending students to the United States. Or, inverting the question, are there certain types of students from a given country who might better be sent to study in France or Switzerland rather than the United States?

The direct involvement of American educational institutions in selection lies in the fact that about 85 percent of the foreign students studying in this country are privately or self-financed. These students frequently make their own arrangements directly with the educational institution in the United States and do not always pass through a screening committee abroad. Whether a student is screened by a selection committee abroad or applies directly to the educational institution, ultimate responsibility for admission rests with the college or university itself. The evaluation of credentials presented by students from abroad requires a highly specialized knowledge not always available in the admitting institution. The United States Office of Education's service in this respect is generally felt to be inadequate because it is both slow and vague.[2]

Certainly, American educational institutions that complain of the caliber of foreign students on their campuses have themselves a serious responsibility in the matter. Not only should they share in establishing selection standards but they should also be cognizant of the best practices of others with experience in this field so that they may bring them to bear on their own screening procedures. The alternative of centralizing the screening of foreign students in a nonacademic institution would entail a questionable abnegation of academic responsibilities. The question of admission procedures will be discussed later.

Quite apart from these considerations, deliberate recruitment is rarely a developed procedure. In the United States, however, the Conference Board of Associated Research Councils has been moving in this direction in the administration of the outbound Fulbright research and teaching personnel. The experience of the highly successful medical training program of the Rockefeller Foundation in India should demonstrate clearly the value of a recruiting program by fellow-professionals. Rockefeller public health doctors who were assigned to work in India for over twenty years selected Indian colleagues for training in the United States. These American-trained men now fill many important posts in India. This type of foreign study program, which is quantitatively small but qualitatively high, has the virtues of

[2] Edward C. Cieslak, "A Study of Administrative and Guidance Practices for Students from Abroad in Representative Collegiate Institutions of the U.S. (Mimeographed; Summary, Ph.D. dissertation, Wayne University, 1953), p. 283.

being professionally directed, of being consistently pursued over time, and of providing continuity of experience.

The matter of selection by competition versus selection by invitation deserves consideration in still another context. In the United States and in many other Western countries competition for awards does not constitute an indignity. But many scholars from Asian countries are offended by the idea of such competitions. Frequently the persons of highest caliber refuse to participate in an impersonal competitive program of this sort. In India, for example, the reluctance of Indian scholars to compete for fifty or sixty awards out of a field of perhaps several thousand applicants is well known to selection committees in that country. Obviously, we are dealing here with a different valuation of what constitutes personal dignity and self-esteem and of the attitude toward competition. Any well-structured selection system should take such differences into account.

The Indian case leads to the further point that presumably each of the best applicants will apply for a fellowship only if he has a fairly high level of assurance that he will receive it. This leads easily into attempts to manipulate committees. Conversely, applicants with less status and influence undoubtedly have a high level of expectation when they apply. There must, therefore, be widespread disappointment to several thousand Indians compared to the gratification felt by only fifty or sixty persons who receive awards. This suggests that the net psychological effect may be a negative one. It might be better to devise a system of appointments based on solicited selection in countries where applicants so far outstrip programmatic resources.

Granting that the ideal situation cannot always be achieved with the instruments at hand, are there nevertheless certain additional considerations based on Part II of this volume that might now be suggested for the selection of students to study abroad? It would appear that emphasis should be placed on an applicant's postreturn opportunities. Questions that might be considered in appraising them are:

Is the applicant breaking his home educational sequence at the right point? For example, is he applying before he enters a university or after he has completed his home university training, or is he breaking into his university training at home?

Is the area of training one which will enhance his life chances in terms of employment, prestige, etc.? For example, will specialization in geriatrics be applicable to medical practice in Afghanistan?

Is the kind of training available in the United States relevant to his return needs? For example, will a Thai agronomist learn more that is relevant to rice culture in the United States or in Japan?

Is the applicant firmly anchored in his home scene? For example, what is the nature and the strength of his family ties, of his patriotism, of his essential peer group? There are obviously no universal criteria for "anchorage" and the significant factors will have to be judged on relevant social and individual considerations.

All of these questions lead clearly in the direction of issues raised earlier—that is, an applicant's potential usefulness to his country and his leadership qualities, but they are now posited in terms that presumably require a sophisticated and consciously directed interview with the applicant rather than only formal records. These considerations are, of course, relevant only to planned programs with formal selection procedures. They cannot and probably should not be applied to the freer flow of self-financed students.

A question of a different order concerns the applicant's language competence. *Is his knowledge of English appropriate to his educational goal?* If there is some question on this score, *is sufficient time allowed for study in the United States to permit him both to acquire greater language competence and to achieve his educational goal?* For example, it may be highly desirable to have a French woman study American social work methods. One year might ordinarily be sufficient. An inadequate command of English should not disqualify her if eighteen months instead of a year of study can be arranged. Frequently the first three months are necessary to make the language adjustment and should be provided for, if all other factors are equal. This suggests strongly that any rigid application of a language competence test is an undesirable measure. Instead, language competence should be judged in part as a function of the intended length of sojourn. (See page 81 ff. for fuller discussion of the language question.)

Until far more is known about the relative effect in different countries of competitive versus invitational selection, about the needs and values of different national groups, about the personal factors that are relatively important or unimportant in the applicant's motives and personality, it may be wise to keep regulations governing selection procedures at a minimum. There may be already too great a tendency to move in the direction of over-generalized standards and procedures on the basis of insufficient evidence.

Prearrival Preparation.—Whether or not a student comes to the United States as a public, private, or self-supported student, prior knowledge of this country has certain meliorating value.

Unfortunately, fellowship grantees too often receive their notification of appointment so late that they cannot adequately prepare for their study sojourn. In a recent study of both Fulbright and the Technical Cooperation Mission grantees in India, 25 percent of those interviewed mentioned hardships in this connection. For example, one person stated, "I had practically given up the idea of going when I got a telegram on August 3, 1951, that I should be prepared to leave Bombay by the 10th and report for the Orientation Course on 6th and 7th." [3] Universities must frequently share responsibility for such delays by sponsoring agencies. Certainly, need for improving the mechanics of these appointments is generally recognized. The same need for improvement in providing inbound students with even rudimentary information about the United States is also recognized. There is no intention here of underlining these important and obvious, if troublesome, procedural matters. [4]

The point which may not be adequately appreciated, however, is the type of predeparture preparation that may prove most useful. When foreign students themselves were consulted on this matter, they gave the following information and opinions in response to a questionnaire addressed in March 1952 to 1,042 first-year State Department grantees. [5]

Two-thirds of the respondents stated that they received information from one or more official sources (United States Information Service, 26 percent; United States Embassies or consulates, 19 percent; local Fulbright committees, 16 percent). It should be remembered that as government grantees, this group was more likely than others to receive official information. Actually, four-fifths of the respondents mentioned unofficial sources of information such as various types of cultural and educational organizations, personal non-American contacts (25 percent), and American visitors abroad (18 percent). Magazines and newspapers were mentioned as sources of unofficial information in 13 percent of the cases. Although many persons

[3] Grace Langley and Sita Basu, "Exchange of Persons: An Evaluation of the Experience and Training of Indian Grantees under Fulbright and TCM Programs," a study prepared for the Evaluation Section of USIA, India, Dec. 1, 1953 (Mimeographed), p. 9.

[4] A preliminary guide to this matter is chap. 4, "Actions To Be Taken Before the Student Arrives," in *Handbook for Counselors of Students from Abroad* (New York: National Association of Foreign Student Advisers).

[5] Bureau of Social Science Research, American University, *An Analysis of First Reports from Foreign Exchange Students: Academic Year 1951–52,* prepared for the Educational Exchange Service, IIA, Dept. of State (Dittoed; Washington, March 1953), pp. 31–40.

are legitimately concerned with the image of America conveyed abroad by motion pictures, it appears that for the student group this medium is not of paramount importance. This is further confirmed by the respondents, who rated the reliability of these sources in descending order as follows: official sources, American visitors, magazines and newspapers, motion pictures.

The chief interest of inbound students, according to this study, was in American society and its way of life (42 percent), in the United States educational system (42 percent), practical living problems (25 percent). Interestingly enough, the adequacy or reliability of the information received was judged to be inverse to their interests. That is, most respondents who felt that their predeparture information had been inadequate believed it to be most so with respect to American society, less so with respect to the United States educational system, and even less so with respect to practical problems. This discrepancy may be explained by the relative complexity of the three areas of interest. Americans (or any other nationals) may find it easier to be articulate and accurate about climate and prices than about institutions and values. This discrepancy may also derive from the fact that precisely the high interest made the coverage seem inadequate.

Finally, when the respondents were asked what they felt were the most important subjects for predeparture briefing of future students, the order of importance again altered. The United States educational system was given highest place (33 percent), practical living problems second place (25 percent), and American society third place (12 percent). The geographic distribution of the respondents who felt that future grantees should be informed about United States customs shows that importance was attached to this topic in ascending order by Latin Americans, Asians, Europeans, and Near and Middle Easterners.

Whatever value may exist in this preliminary study, the best sources of information about the United States and the most important subjects in the minds of foreign students are clearly brought out. Certainly, one of the purposes of predeparture briefing should be to allay uncertainties, or even anxieties, which a student may have as he approaches study abroad. The primary task is to give full and accurate answers to the questions that the applicant feels are most significant, even though they may seem tangential to those who counsel him. It follows from this that the standard published handbooks like *Meet the U.S.A.* may have some virture but cannot do the whole job of predeparture briefing.

However, the study resulting from this guided questionnaire omits a whole field of information of what may constitute one of the most important types of predeparture preparation—knowledge of one's own country. The importance of this question has emerged from both experience and an evaluative study of outbound Americans.

For example, the International Farm Youth Exchange program, which has had many years of carefully planned and supervised exchange experience, urges its American representatives to learn as much as possible about the United States before going abroad. The intent of this recommendation does not go beyond preparing their representatives to meet factual questions that will be asked them. But Hilda Taba's study referred to earlier [6] has gone more searchingly into the implications of this matter. She writes of the American study tour whose learning process she studied:

> It was evident that certain types of orientation facilitated cultural learning. The tour experience suggested that orientation which focuses on methods of analyzing cultures—such as distinguish their universal and unique characteristics—which points out the role of feelings in maintaining and changing cultural values, and that reveals the

[6] Hilda Taba, *Cultural Attitudes and International Understanding: An Evaluation of a Study Tour*, Institute of International Education, Research Program, Occasional Paper No. 5, June 1953 (New York: The Institute).

processes of valid generalization, is more helpful than one limited to specific information about a specific country.

In this connection it appears that knowledge of the dynamics of one's own culture is necessary in order to develop sophistication and detachment concerning cultures in general. Specifically, there is the possibility that Americans going abroad might prepare themselves better by studying American culture rather than the background of the countries they visit. The Tour pointed out that such study could facilitate appreciation of foreign cultures and of international understanding. An orientation to the culture of the United States could also assist in focusing experiences abroad on important cultural differences rather than on surface trivia.

Confirming evidence for this viewpoint comes from both India and Japan. A survey of scholarship students who had returned to Japan after a study sojourn in the United States says that of 153 respondents to a questionnaire, 70 felt able to make a comparison of American and Japanese cultures as a result of their study in the United States and 55 said they had acquired new knowledge about Japanese (their own) culture. Of a hundred suggestions made by Indian subjects as to future orientation courses, one of the most frequently mentioned was that orientation should be given in India and should include more information about India.[7]

Obviously, all foreign students will not be made into cultural anthropologists or comparative sociologists prior to their departure, but national committees or other persons charged with selecting or counseling outbound students can render a considerable service by urging applicants to inform themselves about their own countries and by suggesting as advance reading some of the most valuable social analyses available on the homeland. They might even make questions in this field part of the qualifying interviews and warn students in advance that such will be the case. This suggestion carries with it, of course, the implication that the student counselors themselves

[7] International Education and Culture Association, *Survey of Opinions of GARIOA Scholarship Students Who Studied in U.S.A. in 1952–53* (Tokyo, n.d.), I, 7; and Langley and Basu, *op. cit.*, pp. 26, 71.

should have certain competence in this respect. Certainly American institutions of higher learning might consider the possibility of preparing adequate predeparture briefing materials about American social and cultural life and American values.

Orientation

The student's preparation for study abroad undertaken before departure is only a first step in the continuing sequence of "orientation" involved in cross-cultural study. Orientation on shipboard and on arrival is the next possible step where administrative procedures can facilitate the adjustment of foreign students.

It is generally agreed that some foreign students will benefit greatly from orientation courses given before they undertake their academic work. Such sessions seem most appropriate for those whose English may be deficient, for those whose interests and goals range broadly across the American scene, and for those who need to be informed on the procedures of American educational institutions. They may be less necessary for adults with serious and settled study plans and competent English, but even for them the opportunities should be made available.

The persons responsible for organizing orientation sessions should be prepared to operate them with the greatest possible flexibility. Preliminary scheduling of lectures and other activities may be reassuring and necessary for administrative purposes, but a rigid adherence may be irrelevant or damaging to the self-esteem of the participants. Each member of the group should be sensitively interviewed upon arrival at the orientation center, consulted on his needs as he sees them, and advised about available resources. A foreign student should be made to feel from the beginning that he is appreciated as an individual and that freedom of choice is his. It seems likely that expecting him to answer probing questionnaires at this period may be injudicious. A student may enter the adaptive phase during the orientation sessions and may, therefore, be in one of the most crucial periods of his cross-cultural experience.

Careful procedures at this time may assure a better long-run adjustment. For example, a person sent to "evaluate" an orientation center complained of its being "too free and easy." It proved actually to be a highly effective center for that very reason. So long as a program exists into which foreign students may fit according to *their* needs, where they sense there is available as much support and guidance as *they* feel necessary, the program is likely to be successful.

Many six-week orientation centers have so far been supported primarily by government funds for government fellows.[8] Of 118 collegiate institutions which responded to a survey question on orientation procedures for foreign students, only 34 had a special orientation program or class for incoming students. "The majority of these institutions handled the orientation of foreign students in regular orientation classes, as a part of the special English or speech courses, or by assignment on the 'Big Brother' plan to a student already enrolled." Interestingly enough, only half of the foreign students attending institutions with such facilities reported enrolling in them.[9] Undoubtedly, the quality and intensity of orientation work varies greatly.

Those universities that have not already done so may wish to place their orientation programs on a more assured financial basis than governmental appropriations. Certain institutions

---

[8] In the summer of 1953, 550 foreign students were accommodated in thirteen college and university orientation centers, and 120 were to spend one month's orientation in homes of fourteen American communities. The participating colleges were: Bard, Bennington, Bucknell, Claremont, Columbia, Denver, Duke, Kansas, Mills, Syracuse, William and Mary, Wisconsin, and Yale. For the first time orientation facilities were extended to other than full government fellows. Other fellows included were Ford, Van Leer, and American Olympic Committee. See *Inside IIE* [Institute of International Education], Vol. II, July 24, 1953 (Mimeographed).

[9] Cieslak, *op. cit.*, pp. 288, 289.

that have only a few foreign students may prefer to consolidate preregistration orientation on a regional basis, although this would not be an easy matter to work out administratively. The first problem would be additional stipends for students during the orientation period. If regional centers were systematically developed over several years during which carefully organized records were kept to ensure both cumulative and communicable experience, they could contribute significantly to individual foreign students and at the same time lighten the subsequent task of educators and administrators on the participating campuses.

The program of regional centers would require considerable thought. Many people experienced in orientation work believe that a large group is desirable because it can be broken down into smaller, more evenly matched groups particularly with respect to English language ability. That discussion groups are better than formal lectures is generally claimed. Seasoned American and foreign students are useful participants in orientation centers. Some individuals express a predilection for a group of mixed nationals because the students themselves frequently express satisfaction at meeting people from other countries and because many topics can be discussed with richer comparisons. Others claim that orientation that concentrates on only one or two nationalities allows for a more relevant educational process. It is generally agreed that opportunities to observe American institutions are desirable and that informal hospitality, picnics, camping trips, and the like, are useful. In some institutions the view is expressed that six weeks of orientation prior to registration is less desirable than a briefer initial orientation followed by a program that continues on the campus throughout the year, so that the continuing orientation can be more precisely adjusted to the varying needs of individuals. Some practitioners feel that a brief orientation of not more than four or five days at the port of entry suffices in many cases and that individuals thereafter can be sent directly to their campuses, particularly if the institution provides special counseling services for foreign students.

The Department of State has also experimented with placing its grantees in homes for a month in lieu of the college orientation centers. The Experiment in International Living has been the private contracting agency for this undertaking. Obviously, the placement procedures require the maximum amount of information on the part of the placement agencies, and placement itself must be handled with the greatest delicacy. Undoubtedly, for certain students this device can be more appropriate than college orientation centers although it obviously serves a very different purpose and one less directly relevant to preparation for undertaking academic studies. It is also obvious that an orientation program of this type, if it is to be of high quality, may have to be quantitatively limited.

The relative merits of campus orientation centers and of orientation based on a month in an American home have been discussed in a recent study.[10] The subjects were 55 German students who had received six weeks of orientation at university centers and 98 German students who had been placed for four weeks in homes. It is interesting that the students in each group expressed preference for the type of orientation they had received. The implication may well be that orientation of either type is a satisfactory device to participants. As might be expected, the institutional centers provided gratifying, rational, broad survey-type experiences. The home orientation period was gratifying as an emotional, warm, interpersonal experience. Campus centers proved somewhat more useful in developing the English of those who were most in need of it, although,

---

[10] Department of State, International Educational Exchange Service, "An Orientation Study: The University Centers and the Experiment in International Living Family Program Compared" (Prepared by Evaluation Staff), September 1953 (Mimeographed).

for the 153 Germans involved in this study, the over-all significance of the language problem seems not to have been a major factor. The campus centers provided satisfactory companionship with other foreign students whereas the homes provided warmer ties with Americans. Preliminary indications also are that foreign students whose orientation was in an American family later joined more fully in group activities than did those who attended campus centers.

Whether the campus center or the American family provides the more satisfactory type of orientation is a matter of goals. If formal education is the primary goal of either a foreign student or the institution of higher education, orientation in a campus center seems more appropriate. If the primary goal is to learn about the "American way of life," orientation through family living offers many advantages. (For a further discussion of this point, see pages 178–81.)

Another study provides data on the foreign student's reaction to orientation. Five hundred eighty-four first-year grantees who had not had either university or family-living orientation were asked

... whether they thought such experience "would have been useful." More than half of them thought it would and suggested a variety of reasons; for example, as a "period of adjustment," or "in order to learn the language. . . ." More than a third of the group stated that orientation would *not* have been of much use despite the fact that a leading question in favor of orientation had been put to them. Many went on to explain that the schools which they attended "did all the necessary" for adjustment or that the similarity between the United States and their home country (mostly in the case of British students) precluded such a need, or that they believed adjustment is a "gradual process" and "a personal problem," and cannot be helped along significantly by such expedients.[11]

One final caution may warrant mention. Proponents of no orientation, or of one or another type of orientation, will be able

[11] Bureau of Social Science Research, *Analysis of First Reports, op. cit.,* pp. 50–51.

to marshal evidence in favor of their arguments because few fellowship students, whatever their nationality, will fail to respond courteously and favorably to official or unofficial questionnaires, or even personal interviews.

In sum, orientation, whether in academic centers or in homes, is probably desirable for many students. Either or both types may be superfluous or undesirable to mature and task-centered students. In general, the greater the cultural distance, the more useful orientation may prove. Until there has been far more experience and research in the whole field of cross-cultural education, obligatory orientation is probably undesirable and no one type of orientation should be exclusively encouraged at this time. An experimental approach to orientation procedures should be encouraged for some years to come. This is a task that American colleges and universities might usefully undertake in a systematic fashion, using control groups of both American students and foreign students who have not been given special orientation.

Placement

If satisfactory interpersonal relations and task accomplishment are highly significant factors in the adjustment processes of foreign students, then their placement in the proper kind of American educational institution is crucial. This in turn raises two questions: (1) How many foreign students receive adequate placement counseling? and (2) How satisfactory is guided placement? Answers to these two crucial questions are fragmentary and inconclusive.

The students who received placement assistance from the Institute of International Education in 1953 were as follows: 647 fully paid grantees; 296 Fulbright grantees for whom additional awards had to be found to supplement governmental funds; 244 privately financed students who were referred to the Institute for assistance. This accounts for 1,187 students. In addition, the Institute had supervisory responsibility for 224 "verification" cases, that is, individuals who took up surplus Fulbright travel monies, who made their own contacts with American educational institutions, and whose placements were only verified *post factum* by the Institute. The Institute also had at least 383 "supervision only" cases where it had no share in any placement activity. Presumably, placement and verification were arranged directly from abroad with the American educational institution. The Institute, however, is charged with the usual supervision of such students.

It appears, therefore, that only a fraction of any one year's inbound student group utilizes such placement facilities as the Institute of International Education makes available.

Some light on the second question—How satisfactory is placement?—may be derived obliquely from a questionnaire circulated to 1,042 first-year grantees in 1951–52. Probably two-thirds of the respondents received some placement guidance from the Institute of International Education. Also, they were individuals who presumably had been selected through their binational committees at home. Of the 1,042 respondents, only 8 percent were undergraduates; 88 percent were listed either as graduate or "special" students.[12]

Of the respondents, more than a quarter (286) changed their study plans. Of these, one-third changed their major or minor field of study either because they did not find the work available in the institutions where they were placed or because their interests shifted. It is not possible to judge from the data provided whether the shifts reflect on placement or on selection of candidates. On occasion students from abroad seem to be catalogued in the wrong exchange program. Certainly, the line between trainees, leaders, specialists, and students is hard to draw, and individuals may often find themselves in administra-

[12] *Ibid.*, p. 7.

tive categories that do not meet their needs as well as other existing categories might.

About 5 percent of the sample overtly expressed disappointment with their academic work. The reasons given were that a whole program, an adequate number of courses, or specific courses were not available. In some cases disappointment lay in either the quality of the academic work offered or in the relevance of the work to a non-American environment. But the same difficulties beset American students: they are forced to "shop around" for admission to colleges and universities. They, too, may have to be satisfied with admission to a school that is not their first choice. Advanced students from abroad, in particular, found rigid university requirements such as course work, enforced class attendance, credits, grades, and quizzes often operating at cross-purposes with what they considered their educational goals.

Five percent of the respondents (50) reported that they had abandoned hope of gaining a degree, usually because they did not have enough time in the United States to complete their original plans. It seems likely that the proportion who met with disappointment in this respect was higher than reported and that students who must depend on official support rather than their own funds are more often forced to abandon such goals because of time limits. On the other hand, about an equal number (54) reported that they had raised their sights and expected to gain a degree for which they had not originally planned.[13]

Changes made in academic programs or expressed dissatisfaction with studies in the United States cannot all be attributed to the inadequacy of placement. Despite the human and procedural difficulties that beset this field, one is left with the impression that placement by the Institute of International

[13] The foregoing data are condensed from *Analysis of First Reports . . .*, *ibid.*, pp. 53–59.

Education is satisfactory. But to extract real meaning from this report, there should be control groups of students who are neither officially selected nor aided in placement.

The difficulties of placement are easily listed, but not so easily resolved. Six major placement issues are discussed in the following paragraphs.

First, information available to applicants abroad is inadequate. American consular officers and even information officers cannot be expected to master, or keep abreast of, the complicated and fluctuating scene in American educational institutions. An extensive collection of university and college catalogues in every American consular and diplomatic post has been recommended as an aid. Yet, this would by no means resolve the dilemma of selecting appropriate educational institutions. It might, in fact, only add to an applicant's confusion. It is frequently suggested that before students leave home, they consult United States citizens resident in their country and fellow-nationals who have studied in the United States. Placement advice by well-meaning but uninformed individuals, whether private or official, has been at times the source of considerable confusion and distress. Such advice about place of study, availability of courses in any one year, or the presence of a particular instructor may often be faulty and out of date. Undoubtedly American educational associations or even private institutions could assume some responsibility in this area, including using alumni resident overseas who are kept abreast of changes in their alma mater.

Second, whatever their real needs, foreign students frequently prefer the "name" institutions. Often, those are the only ones known to them. Furthermore, they are also likely to carry the highest prestige on return. Obviously, the preferred "name" institutions cannot absorb the increased numbers of foreign students coming to this country, nor are many of them willing to lower entrance requirements to meet what may appear to be inadequate preparation.

Third, difficulties in placement arise from an inadequate prior knowledge of the capacity, background, and plans of individual applicants as well as of the general academic organization and standards of the candidate's educational institutions. [14] Inadequate information hampers both the outbound and the inbound end of placement activities. If, for example, the student's English is known to be less than adequate, consideration may be given to placing him in a college or university that has specialized in the teaching of English as a foreign language.

Fourth, there is the mechanical difficulty of matching students and grants. Few individual awards cover all the student's expenses. For example, in 1951–52, 16 percent (4,954) of the foreign students in the United States were recipients of more than one type of support. [15] In these cases the various grants and stipends available have to be matched, even if the preferences and educational interests of an individual student may appear to be given less than maximal consideration.

This situation raises the whole complex issue of full versus partial awards. Certainly government aid has greatly stimulated private participation in educational exchanges as an arm of our national cultural relations policy. Partial government awards have been matched by partial private awards. The result has been to increase the over-all number of foreign students who can procure financial aid from American sources. But partial awards whether federal or private have also greatly complicated procedures and paper work, with the result that overhead is probably more costly and time-consuming and that the resulting placement may not meet the best interests of a foreign student.

The present dilemma seems to be that government aid is diminishing as private participation is increasing. On the

[14] Haverford Report, *op. cit.*, p. 22.
[15] *Education for One World, 1951–52* (New York: Institute of International Education, 1952), p. 32.

surface this might be judged an appropriate trend in our national life. But, in fact, the absence of clear planning for such a shift may result in the loss of a certain number of private tuition and maintenance grants because they cannot be supplemented by dollars and counterpart funds. This trend is accentuated by the growing emphasis on full awards in the Department of State's International Educational Exchange Service. Full federal awards concentrate dollar resources on a few students and permit a certain number of private partial awards to go by default. But this very policy entails certain risks, since congressional appropriations of dollars to match counterpart funds cannot be considered assured.

On the one hand, a policy of full federal awards assures financial security and better placement for the small number of government-supported students. On the other hand, a policy of partial federal awards assumes continued "pump-priming" for private but partial matching awards in the form of tuition and maintenance grants. This permits a greater number of foreign students who do not come from economically privileged groups abroad to study in this country. If the Department of State does not encourage the American public to continue partial grants, it may find itself without enough private grants to match its foreign currency resources. This is a dilemma that will not be easily resolved. It is a subject to which the United States Advisory Commission on Higher Education or some comparable group might well direct careful thought.

Fifth, that foreign students should be equitably distributed geographically in the United States is generally accepted. The issue has been raised by congressmen, and probably some of the smaller educational institutions in "remote" sections of the United States have also brought some pressure to bear in this respect. If placement is to stress the needs of the individual students, the criterion of geographic distribution must be considered one of the least relevant. It is difficult, however, to deny the legitimate educational and cultural contribution that American communities and institutions hope to secure from the presence of foreign students. Real conflicts in interests can sometimes arise on this score and complicate placement procedures.

Sixth, educational institutions which criticize foreign student placement are sometimes themselves culpable. Their delays in replying to Institute of International Education placement queries frequently jeopardize matching student and opportunity to best advantage. [16] In addition, they may give less than well-informed and dispassionate consideration to the applicant's needs.

These are difficulties that will not be quickly, easily, and wholly overcome. They can be met in part through experience and continuing, conscientious effort, but they cannot be met through administration that is broad scale and mechanically imposed.

This raises the final issue in respect to placement, namely, the desirability of a centralized placement bureau. So long as public and private partial awards continue to exist, a central resource can render valuable service. However, the quality of its services will depend upon having early and full information both here and abroad, up-to-date information in placement files toward which educational institutions and private scholars must feel some obligation, and prompt responses by university administrators on matters submitted to them. Such a service should be available for a fee to both private students from abroad and to American educational institutions. It need hardly be stressed that these services would be optional and advisory only. The ultimate responsibility of the individual American educational institution for admitting foreign students is a right that must

---

[16] An analysis of Institute of International Education placements for 1953 indicates that a total of 376 student applications, or about 22 percent of all applications sent out, were held for two months or longer by the educational institutions receiving them (Institute of International Education, *The Reporter*, Dec. 11, 1953, p. 2).

be rigorously protected. At the same time foreign students should be given the opportunity and encouraged to make intelligent choices of their own in applying to American educational institutions. Ideally, every foreign student coming to the United States, whether privately or publicly financed, should have adequate advance counseling and should be urged to utilize available placement resources; but, whatever the type of financing, his freedom of choice should be as zealously safeguarded as practical considerations permit.

Admission Standards and Procedures.—Whatever the difficulties of placement may be from the viewpoint of administrative agencies, final decisions for placement rest with the admission personnel of American educational institutions themselves. The admission of foreign students is a complex responsibility. The heterogeneity of American institutions of higher education is apparent in admission standards and procedures as it is in all other aspects of their educational functions.

The most useful survey of admission standards and procedures known to the writer is that of Dr. Cieslak of Wayne University, [17] who obtained his data from responses to questionnaires sent to 122 schools and 354 students. Dr. Cieslak believes these responses constitute a good sample. The following findings derive from this report.

(1) It appears that foreign student advisers are only infrequently consulted on admission of foreign students. (2) There is a tendency to devise special forms and informational materials for foreign students. (3) There seems to be a relationship between the group of students who received the least number of informational materials and the group that was under the sponsorship of a noncollegiate agency. (4) The rank-order of qualifications for admission considered desirable for foreign students by the 122 responding institutions is: (*a*) sufficient

[17] Edward C. Cieslak, *op. cit.*

mastery of English; (*b*) adequate financing; (*c*) superior academic record; (*d*) certificate of admission to a homeland university; (*e*) certificate of health; (*f*) testimonials of character; (*g*) plans to return home; (*h*) satisfactory score on College Board Entrance Examinations or their equivalent; (*i*) Christian faith; (*j*) interest in extracurricular activities or practical experience in nonacademic work; and (*k*) athletic skill. (5) Admission by examination is rare, and opinions are divided on the desirability of such examinations. (6) Ninety-one percent of the sample will admit foreign students who are already in the country on a student visa but who have not yet attended the school of admission. Actually, 92 students, or 38 percent of the respondents in this sample, were admitted without filling out an application form.

This list of findings presents a generalized indictment of admission policies and procedures of American academic institutions, although an examination would disclose a wide variation of practices. For example, some state-supported institutions are required by law to admit any student who presents even quite low qualifications. Although these laws are intended for residents of the state, as written they apply also to foreign students. Obviously, university administrative officers need to arrive at a code of minimum standards for admission of foreign students to various types of schools, but this does not mean that standards should be uniform for all schools or for all foreign students, nor that procedures should be minutely regulatory.

Another weakness of the present handling of foreign students seeking admission to higher institutions is that rarely does an institution have a system for advising or referring refused applicants; actually any system of this kind would require manpower and competence beyond the reach of most of them. An alternate possibility is that a central agency assume responsibility for assisting rejected applicants, but this solution—which has been suggested in the past—faces, among other obstacles, the complication of its relationships with educational institutions.

These questions lead to the consideration in the next chapter of actual policies and practices of institutions in dealing with foreign students on campuses and the reasons underlying them.

Conclusions

The present procedures for selecting students from abroad leave room for improvement, both when foreign selection committees assist and when the arrangements are made by direct correspondence between the individual and the American institution. Proper selection is made the more difficult—if not impossible—if inadequate or inappropriate information is given about the candidate, about foreign educational systems, or about American educational resources. American educational institutions have both an interest and an obligation to provide a flow of revelant and up-to-date information to institutions abroad and to central public and private agencies in the United States.

Even if selection has been judicious, predeparture briefing of students, including early notification of placement, is important. They need especially objective statements about the American educational system and about American values and social organization. And here again, our colleges and universities could stimulate more and better efforts. For certain categories of students, orientation programs of various kinds, presented upon their arrival in this country, are advantageous—and benefit as well the institutions in which they will study. As yet, however, there are no clear-cut criteria for identifying the type of student who needs orientation nor the kind of orientation best adapted to the needs of both student and institution. Systematic study and experimentation along these lines is needed.

The placement of students by administrative agencies is a complex problem in which many interests must be served, including those of colleges and universities. Educational administrators have both an interest and responsibility in this respect: they need to have a sympathetic and thorough understanding of the procedures, and they should have facilities for prompt and efficient processing of all inquiries.

Ultimate responsibility for placement properly rests with the admissions officers of the colleges and universities. Explicit and informed policies concerning the standards of admission for foreign students, widely disseminated both within each institution and to relevant outside agencies, would expedite the bringing of the proper foreign students to the appropriate American campus.

Basic throughout is competent fact-finding by the educational associations. And until the facts are collected, the formulation of tight administrative regulations should be avoided. Fact-finding in this instance requires planning and continuity of investigation on each campus as well as a reliable system of communication with others who select and place students. The heterogeneity of our institutions, the number of noneducational organizations involved, and the number of countries whose youth come to this country all conspire to complicate the practical aspects of administration and suggest both caution and diversity in the solutions sought.

Chapter **12**

CAMPUS POLICIES
AND PRACTICES

ATTITUDES in American universities toward foreign students range from ignoring "foreignness," at least on an official level, to treating the foreign student as a *rara avis* and making him the coddled or lionized pet of campus and community. These are the extremes; fortunately customary practice falls short of both.

Assimilation

The great and ancient universities of Europe are international centers, both by origin and tradition. They grew up in a period when nationalism was still in its infancy, when the Christian world and the Latin language provided a common basis for communication among scholars. The interchange of learning and of scholars was an accepted practice.

Some American universities, particularly some of the older private ones, have inherited this tradition. The old internationalism of scholarship and the new internationalism of science are still paramount in these institutions. Because of their distinguished reputations they are often the ones that have the largest enrollment of foreign students. By and large they are

165

also the universities that believe scholarship and learning must be self-motivated and pursued by mature people. These institutions tend not to be self-consciously concerned about *the* foreign student.

Many other American colleges, and particularly the state and land-grant universities, are rooted in a philosophy of educational obligations to the local citizenry.[1] Until recently, their principal contacts with "foreignness" in the student body were through first- or second-generation foreigners, and assimilation was an aim in their education. The assimilation of the foreign-born has been one of the outstanding achievements and traditions of the American nation, and like all such traditional achievements, it is not easily abandoned. But today the relationship to foreign students sojourning in this country can no longer be based on that tradition. Assimilation is neither generally desired by the foreign students themselves nor is it in accordance with the laws governing their entrance into this country. However, the important goal of education for citizenship deemed appropriate to the American undergraduate is inevitably and often unconsciously extended to foreign students.

Whereas the state university may drift toward assimilation unless conscious effort to the contrary is exercised, certain sectarian schools (and even some officially listed as nonsectarian) have assimilation to American life as a conscious goal. Assimilation may be phrased as either Christian or cultural proselytizing. For example, one committee (that discretion prevents naming), after making several recommendations to strengthen the role of the foreign student adviser, states, "Such a program . . .

[1] " . . . most European universities content themselves with being in the first place repositories of knowledge and centers of teaching and of research, mainly research by individual scholars. The idea prevalent in the United States that universities have an important task in making their students better citizens is not entirely absent from the European mind, but less prominent. . . ." Jan Barents, "University of Amsterdam and World Affairs," in *Universities and World Affairs*, Doc. 22, Sept. 15, 1953, p. 2 (issued by the Carnegie Endowment for International Peace).

might well disintegrate the barriers of caste [sic] and accelerate the assimilation that is so necessary for the prevention of a heightened anti-Americanism." The cultural imperialism of such a statement is at the opposite pole from the internationalism of the traditional university system.

Student Counseling

The aspect of the American educational philosophy which deals with producing good citizens deserves further consideration, for its ramifications are numerous. In our democracy, the electorate, in which political power is ultimately vested, is required to pass judgment on problems that have become increasingly complex. It has been assumed that the extension of the educational period will help to produce an electorate that is able to solve problems intelligently and is prepared for responsible and practical action. Education, therefore, tends to stress problems and problem-solving rather than the production of an intellectual elite.

As discussed earlier, we in America are more preoccupied with the welfare of the individual than the cultivation of individualism. These factors interact to foster the counseling and guidance of students in every phase of their personal as well as their intellectual lives. The more standardized the education and the more elaborate the institution, the more individual counseling seems necessary to fit diverse human beings into the requirements of our highly structured group life. Those who plead the value of self-reliance and independence to learn— even though this means painful experience and "wasted" time and opportunities—are in a growing minority in the contemporary American scene.

It is in such an educational milieu that many foreign students find themselves. And to most Americans it appears that if they are to function within the framework of our predominant educational philosophy, their need for counseling is particularly acute.

Whether the "spoon-feeding" taken so for granted by American students is in fact desirable or acceptable to many foreign students is certainly debatable. However, if they are here to observe and even to participate in the American educational scene, it would be a falsification of that scene and an act of discrimination not to provide them with facilities at least equivalent to those provided American students.

Accepting the existence of a large corps of people who are convinced of the importance of the specialized field of foreign student counseling, the following remarks will be turned in that direction. The experience of thousands of officially designated foreign student counselors and of faculty and staff members who have unofficially counseled foreign students through their educational sojourn in the United States deserves far more study than has been here invested in the subject. The *Handbook for Counselors of Students from Abroad* [2] goes far in bringing together both the practical knowledge and the experience of such individuals. The writer has no desire to review this contribution although the hope is that it may soon be revised and brought up to date.

In another sense, Part Two of the present volume bears on the dynamics of personal adjustment that form a part of the daily problems faced by foreign student advisers and by administrators. Even a casual inquiry into the field of foreign student counseling reveals that there are still many questions that might usefully be posed.

The first useful distinction is between what might be called advice and counseling. The *Handbook* refines this distinction

[2] *Handbook for Counselors of Students from Abroad,* Experimental Edition, 1949, prepared by members of the Practicum for Foreign Student Advisers, Teachers College, Columbia University, Summer Session, 1948 (New York: National Association of Foreign Student Advisers, n.d.).

into "information, advice, and counseling." Here, however, "advice" is used to cover the innumerable practical and inescapable facts about which virtually all foreign students need information—immigration regulations, finances, insurance plans, details of living in this country, units, credits, requirements, and the like. The need for information on many of these subjects is urgent among both Americans and foreign students, although for foreign students the range is greater and the information will not be so readily grasped. This suggests the need for greater effort with respect to foreign students. Although there is no intention here to dwell on these obvious informational matters, there is also no intention of minimizing their importance. All that has gone before underlines sharply the need to put such material at the disposal of our foreign guests clearly and early in the course of their plans to study in the United States. Many publications of varying worth and timeliness already exist to fill such needs. [3]

"Counseling," as distinguished from advice, is used here to cover not only the manner in which advice is imparted but also guidance in the personal dilemmas and confusions that often carry deep emotional undertones, as well as overtones, for individual foreign students.

Program or academic counseling is an obvious point of departure. Foreign students arrive on a campus variously prepared for what they will encounter. Some may have had excellent advice precisely geared to their expectations and to the resources of the institution in which they register. Others may have been improperly advised. Or, the advice concerning the institutional resources may have been correct but those resources may not fit the student's expectations and needs. Others may arrive on

[3] Only a few examples are included here in addition to the National Association of Foreign Student Advisers' *Handbook* previously alluded to and the International Institute of Education's *Meet the U.S.A., Study in the U.S.A.,* and *Graduate Study in the U.S.A.*

a campus completely unadvised and with only vaguely formulated expectations and needs. Each student will require
academic guidance, and for each student the guidance will
differ in quality, depth, and understanding according to his
situation. Unfortunately, his arrival on campus will probably
coincide with the confusion of registration and when many of
the faculty consultants are still absent. Too often registration
and consultation are assigned to overworked and/or junior
persons.

The temptation is to "throw the book" at the student, whether
foreign or American. Although the foreign student's past record
had already been scrutinized at the time he was admitted, there
is no assurance that the judgment then exercised is transmitted
to the individuals on the campus who guide the student through
the selection of courses and registration. The case of a student
from Nepal who, after spending several years studying English,
was told by her adviser that she had no foreign language and
must, therefore, study French for two years, is only an isolated
instance of the insistence on formal requirements at the expense
of constructive academic guidance. If the frequently rigid
and cumbersome regulations of our larger institutions are not
to be arbitrarily applied to the detriment of individual students,
academic counseling must not be entrusted to poorly informed,
overworked, careless, or rigid personalities. The most careful
advance scheduling is needed to assure that foreign students
will receive the attention required at this crucial stage in their
American academic sojourn. The task-oriented students, with
very definite career objectives, often are the most sensitive to
decisions made at this stage.

Counseling that is concerned with emotional dilemmas is,
necessarily, more difficult and subtle than that dealing with
immediate educational issues. It relates intimately to some of
the common, yet significant factors, discussed earlier, that
foreign students face in the course of cross-cultural education.

Among these, the importance of at least one warm and reliable relationship in meeting these dilemmas has been stressed earlier. While a designated foreign student counselor on a campus cannot be expected to fulfill this role except in an occasional instance, and while it would be presumptuous to dictate or advise counselors as to whom they should choose as friends or protégés, they may be alerted to the often acute need of many foreign students for a warm, supportive relationship. The very role of counselor, like that of a therapist, makes him the natural and accessible source for such emotional support. He needs to be aware of the importance of such a relationship and to do whatever he can to facilitate its establishment elsewhere rather than to attempt to fulfill the need himself. It is probably the better part of wisdom for the counselor to refrain from undertaking, or promising to undertake, roles that he is incapable of carrying through in relation to particular students.

Varying Functions of Advisers.—This raises the question of the functions that foreign student advisers can or should undertake. The answer will depend to a large extent upon the local campus and the particular individual concerned. The larger and more complex the institution, the more important becomes individual counseling. Such counseling becomes a device that compensates for the impersonality and elaborate managerial structure of our large institutions. On a campus with perhaps not more than a dozen foreign students, a single faculty member assigned part time to these duties is capable of considerable individual counseling. But even under these circumstances, it seems desirable to have a parallel person in the administration whose responsibility is to be fully informed on the regulations and conditions governing students from abroad. The function of personal counselor can probably be more constructively discharged if it is divorced from the function of enforcing official regulations.

We have assumed that the faculty adviser in this situation

is a person who is seriously devoted to foreign student counseling and finds the task rewarding in itself. Unfortunately, however devoted such faculty members may be, their counseling duties often conflict with their professional aspirations and careers. Student counseling rarely brings professional recognition and academic promotions. If faculty members are released from a certain amount of teaching in order to counsel foreign students, both the adviser and his department may suffer as a result, and the temptation arises to rotate the task among different individuals and departments. In such a situation, the wisdom that comes only from experience is repeatedly squandered. The responsibility of the administration and of the faculty to their colleagues in this situation is clear.

On a larger campus or one on which foreign students may number a hundred or more, the need for a full-time adviser who is responsible for foreign student affairs becomes more evident. The complicated minutiae that beset foreign student affairs are often eagerly placed on the shoulders of such an officer, who is generally a member of the administrative staff rather than of the faculty. This, too, has its drawbacks. A foreign student adviser in this context may be able to provide the needed advice, but he can scarcely be expected to discharge competently the individual academic and personal counseling that may be required. His mere presence on the campus may encourage a busy faculty to assign tasks to him that properly they cannot or should not dodge. It then becomes the adviser's job to persuade the faculty to assume their appropriate roles. This is often no easy undertaking, particularly in view of the relative status of faculty members and foreign student advisers.

With the establishment of a foreign student advisory service and an increase in the numbers of foreign students, there may also develop a variety of community relationships, responsibility for which usually centers in the adviser's office. Useful and desirable as such community activities may be, there is always the risk that the means will take precedence over the ends. This preoccupation is reflected, for example, in the experience of 132 Indian trainees and Fulbright students. Fifty-three percent reported that their social contacts in the United States had been of a community type whereas only 29 percent reported personalized contacts with families.[4] Foreign student advisers run the risk of having organized social contacts like picnics, dances, discussion groups, local tours, and home hospitality become for them time-consuming and engrossing ends in themselves. The individual guidance that aims to assist foreign students to establish the right kind of personal relationships may become secondary or incidental to entertainment and participation for its own sake. Gregariousness and group activities are given high value in American life, and foreign students may wish to observe and even participate in this aspect of our national existence. But the mistake is in supposing that gregariousness is an equivalent of supportive interpersonal relations. Too great immersion in these social activities, particularly early in the sojourn, may serve only to increase the students' bewilderment. Moreover, acceptance of frequent invitations may make the student feel that he is obliged to reciprocate for even the most freely given hospitality.

On campuses where no organizational provision is made for foreign student counseling, the administrative offices may provide competent advice and centralized records and information. The administration expects that both the faculty and the student body will assume voluntarily the obligations of host to the stranger in their midst. Each campus that operates on such a philosophy must itself determine whether this is in fact the case. But in any large institution, particularly in an urban setting, such an assumption is suspect.

[4] Grace Langley and Sita Basu, "Exchange of Persons: An Evaluation of the Experience and Training of Indian Grantees under Fulbright and TCM Programs," a study prepared for the Evaluation Section of USIA, India, Dec. 1, 1953 (Mimeographed), p. 62.

Carried one step further, such a philosophy may be phrased in terms of "students are students." The reasoning behind such a position runs somewhat as follows: "American students have much the same problems as foreign students; foreign students may avail themselves of advice as freely as the Americans; those that are related to the Institute of International Education already get outside assistance; the Institute should extend its services to all foreign students who have special problems; this is an educational institution; its task is to get on with education; it is not set up to do social work."

There is undoubtedly some virtue in this position, particularly for mature students who are well placed and task-oriented. Certainly, every campus, whatever its administrative arrangements for handling foreign students, should recognize that this philosophy is congenial to a certain proportion of all students from abroad and there is no need to insist on counseling when it is neither needed nor wanted. Nevertheless, there is usually a certain number of foreign students on any campus for whom intelligent and sensitive counseling may make the difference between a personally constructive or destructive sojourn. Too often, in a situation of this type Americans with a special ax to grind may step in, and in the process do as much harm as good— however lofty their intentions.

Qualifications of Advisers.—The qualifications of those who counsel foreign students, whether professionally or nonprofessionally, as well as methods of counseling have been excellently summarized in *Handbook for Counselors of Students from Abroad.* [5] However, the statement of qualifications occasionally evidences certain unconscious cultural determinants. At the risk of appearing both presumptuous and hypercritical, a few points have been selected for comment here. For example, to what extent can the professional counselor really function as a

[5] *Op. cit.*, pp. 128–53.

friend, however friendly his feelings may be? This point has been raised earlier. Although planned activities may be necessary, is there not some risk that the planning may become so important in the adviser's eyes that unwillingness to go along with plans may be seen by him as rejection and a "problem"? The stress on group activities, sharing, and participation are not valued in all countries to the degree that they are in the United States. Although the students should feel that avenues to this kind of activity are open to them, there should certainly be no pressure, however indirect, to force participation. Also, the philosophy of permissive counseling that is so widely approved in this country may only be confusing and distressing to a student who is accustomed to looking for, and needs, more firmly structured guidance. Particularly in the early part of his sojourn a student may be in no position to "assume the moral obligation for decision and action." Furthermore, he may experience considerable confusion between the areas in which he encounters unexpectedly rigid regulations and areas in which he encounters equally unexpected latitude for self-determination.

In the same *Handbook for Counselors* the qualifications for foreign student advisers, although admirable, are ideal rather than practical. For example, it suggests that a knowledge of American culture and of the chief characteristics of the cultures of the world is desirable. That counselors have such knowledge may be desirable but hardly realizable. More nearly practical might be the suggestion that the counselor have some grasp of the concepts of cultural relativism and of the relationship between personality and culture. This would also serve to place in perspective his knowledge of the principles and techniques of counseling that are derived from the American social setting.

The suggestion that one put oneself in the place of a foreign student seeking help from a counselor, while admirable in suggesting the importance of empathy, should at least carry a word of caution on the subject of projection. If any exception is taken to a statement of ideal qualification, it is that a wide and even unbridgeable gap between goals and performance can produce psychological difficulties in foreign student counselors as well as in foreign students. It may be wiser to set qualifications more nearly within the realm of the achievable.

With the authors of the *Handbook* one can agree that the counselor must above all avoid being a deculturated individual. Of him it should not be possible to say, "The person who finds most interest in talking to foreigners and giving up his time to them is likely to be a person who for some reason or the other does not find adequate satisfactions in his own position in his own society." [6]

Cultural and Educational Attachés.—In the counseling of foreign students, cultural and educational attachés are a potential off-campus resource that has not been adequately developed. The bursary students of foreign countries are usually under some degree of supervision by their embassies. In many countries where dollar exchange is controlled, even self-supporting students who study in the United States are a source of concern to their governments since dollars are released to them for educational purposes. As a result, some of the educational or cultural attachés of these countries may evince considerable interest in the performance of their nationals studying in American institutions. Frequently such officials, who are identified with national interests as they envisage them, may evince a degree of rigidity concerning fields of study and academic performance that is not always consonant with the educational development of the individual student as conceived by American advisers. It has been suggested that in the case of such disparities the role of the foreign student advisers should be that of advocate for the foreign student. Perhaps the more judicious role would be that of go-between.

[6] Geoffrey Gorer, "National Character: Theory and Practice," in Margaret Mead and Rhoda Metraux, *The Study of Culture at a Distance* (Chicago: University of Chicago Press, 1953), p. 164.

In a larger sense there is a broad, if difficult, task to be performed by educational attachés. A "good" attaché from the American educational point of view would be one who knows his own and the American educational system, who is free to travel in the United States to visit his fellow-nationals on various campuses, who stays abreast of educational developments in his home country, and who has sufficient authority to act without referring routine administrative decisions to his home government. In this last instance, sometimes delays caused by referral to home governments have resulted in uncertainties detrimental to all concerned.

Ideally, the educational attaché should function as an intermediary between the student and his homeland by keeping him in touch with national developments and interests. With tact and sympathy he can do much to counteract the possible alienation of certain individuals. He should also be prepared to help foreign student advisers in problems of counseling that involve cross-cultural differences. His role in making his country's educational system known to American educators and particularly those charged with admission procedures for foreign students could be highly constructive. He should be prepared to exercise authority in sending a student home when that course is clearly indicated. But contrariwise, he should also be prepared to solicit financial and other assistance from fellow-nationals when need for such aid is called for. Educational attachés may often be in a position to tap resources and reach persons both beyond the campus and on the campus that are not accessible to foreign student advisers.

In sum, the cultural attaché if appropriately selected and if constructively related to foreign student affairs in the United States can be a resource of great value. Such a role, however, requires that these posts be filled by persons genuinely devoted to education and not by diplomats who may consider the office as a bypath on the main road of their careers.

Here again the educational officers of American colleges and universities have an opportunity to bring creative influence to bear by relating themselves actively and constructively to the cultural and educational attachés stationed in Washington, D.C. The *Diplomatic List* [7] furnishes the names of all such officers. Their visits to American campuses should prove useful, and their advice in special cases should be solicited.

Living Arrangements

In addition to the attitudes toward and provisions for counseling foreign students, the living arrangements considered appropriate for them are a sensitive index to the general philosophy that prevails in any given institution. There are several well-rationalized convictions concerning what constitutes the proper living arrangements for students from abroad.

There are those who believe that foreign students should be housed like American students. They are either assigned to dormitories or given local rooming house lists. The rationale of this position is that, if nonnationals come to the United States to experience life in this country, they should be given the opportunity to see it as it is. Critics of this position point out that actually foreign students may suffer handicaps of language, color, know-how, and community prejudices that American students either do not suffer or have learned to cope with. For young students, dormitories or fraternities may well provide opportunities to establish warm personal relationships with students of the same age group and having comparable interests. For older men, dormitory life particularly on the more "spirited" campuses can verge on the intolerable. Where rooming houses or apartments are suggested, there is some likelihood that nationals will cluster together.

There are proponents of international houses for foreign stu-

---

[7] Washington: Government Printing Office, bimonthly; $0.20.

dents. The rationale is that students can there find not only fellow-nationals but other persons who may be sharing the same experiences, and from such common experiences they may find mutuality and support as well as pleasant surroundings. Proponents of international houses also underline the values of an international as opposed to the binational atmosphere of such quarters. The American student, resident in the house, benefits from this atmosphere of internationalism as much as the non-national. Critics of international houses say that they breed national cliques, that they serve as an obstacle to fuller and deeper contacts with American life, that the American student who is attracted to the international houses is often a marginal individual.

There is also a very widespread opinion that living with an American family is the most desirable housing arrangement for foreign students. The reason most frequently advanced is that it permits the student to learn more about the "real" life of Americans.

It is interesting in the face of these varied opinions to examine what we know of housing for foreign students and the satisfaction felt by them with their living quarters. A study in 1951–52 of 1,042 students, all recipients of Department of State grants and all in their first year of residence in the United States, revealed the following:

Nearly half of the grantees live in dormitories; another 10 percent occupy other university-connected lodgings such as fraternity houses, International Houses, and, in the case of medical students, hospital quarters. Of the 383 grantees who live off-campus, 107 live with families, and the rest in apartments, boarding houses, furnished rooms, etc.

More than half of all the students share their quarters with others, about half of them with American students. If the 107 who live with families (presumably American) are added to this number, it appears that 41 percent (431) of all grantees lodge in some kind of close contact with Americans.

Most students seem to find their living quarters acceptable. Less than 4 percent (38 cases) rate them unsatisfactory, the most frequent reason being that they are crowded, dirty, or noisy. Nearly two-thirds (59 percent) check "adequate" (in reply to a questionnaire on the subject) and more than a third (35 percent), "excellent."

Those who live with families appear to be most pleased: 47 percent of them rate their quarters as "excellent," compared with 38 percent of those living in dormitories, and only 23 percent of those who rent apartments or private rooms.

Europeans tend, as a group, to be most often pleased with their living arrangements: 41 percent rate them as "excellent" (54 percent say "adequate"), compared with 25 percent of the Latin Americans (60 percent "adequate"), and 10 percent of the Near and Middle East grantees (86 percent "adequate").[8]

As the writers point out, the varying values attached to the words "excellent" and "adequate" do not provide an objective basis for comparing true satisfaction. Furthermore, the factor of courtesy must also be taken into consideration in weighing the significance of these responses. Although greater satisfaction may in fact derive from living in homes, there is also greater pressure for courtesy in such replies.

Another factor must also be taken into consideration in appraising the answers to this questionnaire—and in fact to most such questionnaires. If the four stages of adjustment suggested in Part II are valid, replies will vary according to the phase of adjustment through which students are passing. It has been suggested that adjusting to a family only heightens emotional strain during the adaptive phase. Certain experienced advisers believe that living with an American family should come only later in the sojourn and should be arranged through mutual selection. For example, in one educational institution, foreign students are given the opportunity to spend a week end with a family during the orientation period. As the semester progresses, group functions are arranged, such as picnics, to

[8] Bureau of Social Science Research, American University, *An Analysis of First Reports from Foreign Exchange Students: Academic Year 1951–52*, prepared for the Educational Exchange Service, IIA, Dept. of State (Dittoed; Washington, March 1953).

which American families are invited. If, in the course of the year, American families and foreign students establish relationships spontaneously and the foreign student finds a substitute home with his American family, the procedure is considered to have succeeded. However, at no time are such relationships forced.

Residence in a home should provide the interpersonal satisfaction deemed so important in Part II, if the persons involved prove congenial and the student is admitted to family life. However, by the same token, such residence can be proportionally damaging and isolating if the persons involved prove uncongenial and if the student is excluded from family life. There can obviously be no categorical answer to the various opinions about housing and none should be attempted. What the data suggest is that particular attention to living arrangements should be given Near and Middle Eastern, Latin-American, and Asian students, in that order of priority.

"Dating" and Married Students

Another point in connection with living conditions is closely associated with the question of sex. Undoubtedly, many foreign students find not only our "dating" customs baffling in different ways and for different reasons, but there are repeated indications that this is an area of considerable maladjustment. There is need for careful study on this subject although the possibility of ameliorative action is probably minimal. There is, however, one suggestion frequently made by the students themselves that deserves more serious consideration than it generally receives. This is the question of bringing wives to this country.

We do not know how many of the foreign students in the United States are married. It may be assumed that a considerable number of them are married, since 42 percent of them are between twenty and twenty-five, and another 33 percent are over twenty-five years of age.

Here again, many opinions and factors enter the picture. Certainly, the major impediment to having wives accompany foreign students is a financial one. This factor applies to students who come on their own funds as well as to those receiving public or private assistance. So far as public or even private assistance is concerned, this is an understandable regulation. However, some dissatisfaction has been expressed on the discriminatory aspects of the Fulbright outbound advanced awards, since American professors and researchers are given maintenance stipends for up to four accompanying dependents (but not travel allowances).

The importance of having wives accompany husbands has been variously argued. Points raised in favor of having wives accompany their husbands are that: it permits the student a normal sexual life; it avoids the risk of alienating spouses; it increases the number of persons exposed to American life; it facilitates psychological adjustment to this country. The main point raised against bringing wives, other than the practical financial one, is that married couples more easily isolate themselves from the American scene. It has been claimed that in some cases wives whose English is inadequate and whose educational background is limited hinder their husbands' studies and social contacts.

Academic Status

In the consideration so far given to the practices and policies of American educational institutions with respect to foreign students, little has been said of their primary function, that of formal education. In this connection, credits and academic status become salient issues.

The evaluation of foreign credentials is undoubtedly one of the most perplexing questions faced by American educational institutions. From what has been said earlier on the subject of policy and procedures for selection, placement, and admission, it is clear that most educational institutions do, and should, take responsibility for evaluating the student records sent them. It is equally clear that academic records from foreign educational institutions are difficult to appraise and are often treated casually among the various factors taken into consideration when admitting foreign students. The United States Office of Education's Division of International Education is widely criticized for not acting with sufficient dispatch and precision in providing required services to educational institutions in this respect. In actual practice, American educational institutions show wide variation in their evaluation of foreign credentials. This situation reflects widespread uncertainty among admissions officers about the value of credentials submitted to them and on the comparative standards of American and foreign educational systems. It also reflects the varying academic standards to which American educational institutions aspire.

The result of this situation is that a large number of institutions tend to admit foreign students on either probationary status or as "special students." In the 1951–52 census of foreign students, more than 2,600 students, or 8.5 percent, were listed as unclassified (special).[9] Our incapacity to evaluate credentials properly tends to heighten the natural insecurities felt by many foreign students on entering a new educational system.

Although there is need for serious attention to this matter by American educators and educational administrators, it should also be recognized that this question of accreditation is not a problem unique to the United States. The variety and autonomy of our educational institutions and the standards they maintain serve to confuse other nations even more than they do us. As a result, American credits and degrees abroad are frequently given little attention. This is not only a disadvantage to American

[9] Institute of International Education, *Education for One World, 1951–52* (New York: The Institute, 1952), p. 23.

students abroad but also to the nationals who return with American degrees. For example, in the Social Science Research Council's study of the readjustment problems of returned students, the research workers for Sweden, Mexico, and Japan all reported the difficulties met by returning nationals in securing official recognition for their American studies. American institutions of higher learning would render an important service by suggesting how best to provide a central service for current and accurate information on accreditation both in this country and abroad.

Academic Performance

Whatever complexities may exist in the selection, placement, and academic status of foreign students entering the American educational system, their academic performance is presumably the final test of the efficacy of these procedural matters and of the American system of teaching. Yet, any discussion of the academic achievement of foreign students is fraught with difficulties. Can academic achievement be examined "objectively" in terms of a quantitative study of grade records? If so, how does one allow for the vastly different standards between American academic institutions or even between instructors within institutions? It is freely admitted that instructors vary considerably in the leniency they show individual foreign students, not only in grading but also in the amount of personal effort they make to carry foreign students who are handicapped in preparatory training, language, "intelligence," or social adjustment. Furthermore, how does one select an American control group so that a comparison can be made between American and foreign students?

Recent studies of foreign student grades do not meet all of these points but do serve to cast some preliminary light on the academic records of students from abroad.

Of 633 Department of State affiliated students 37 percent reported an average grade of A; 57 percent reported an average grade of B; and only 6 percent reported an average grade of C or below.[10] When these grades are compared with those in a study by the Association of Graduate Schools,[11] one might conclude that government-affiliated students are more carefully selected for scholastic ability than is the average foreign student in the United States. However, the majority of government-affiliated students are at the graduate level. A grade of C in many graduate schools is considered a serious warning to advanced students and is given more sparingly than on the undergraduate level. One is therefore somewhat at loss to know how to evaluate comparatively the two available studies.

Turning now to the study by the Association of Graduate Schools, their findings can be summarized as shown in Table 1.

TABLE 1

SCHOLASTIC RECORDS OF FOREIGN STUDENTS BY
MAJOR WORLD REGIONS *

AREA	ABOVE AVERAGE		BELOW AVERAGE		TOTAL NO. OF CASES SPECIFIED
	No.	Percent	No.	Percent	
Europe..........	213	44	88	20	437
Far East..........	314	32	221	24	902
Near East........	118	38	73	24	308
Latin America.....	43	22	68	37	182
Total..........	688	38	430	24	1,829

* Africa and the British Commonwealth students are each omitted, for different reasons

When one considers these figures by countries, there are eleven out of fifty-four whose student population is 30 percent

[10] Bureau of Social Science Research, American University, *Foreign Exchange Students Review Their Stay in the United States: An Analysis of Second Semester Reports, Academic Year 1951–52*, prepared for the Evaluation Staff, International Educational Exchange Service, Dept. of State, August 1953 (Mimeographed), p. 10.

[11] Association of Graduate Schools, *Report of the Committee on Problems of Foreign Students*, 1953 (Mimeographed).

or more below average. As might be expected from the foregoing table, most of these countries are in the Far Eastern or Latin-American regions. One astonishing exception is Norway with a representation of twenty-six students in the sample, of whom nine, or 35 percent, are reported as below average. When one considers Europe as a whole, it is also astonishing to find 20 percent rated as below average in view of the "advanced" educational systems of Europe, the greater ease in evaluating their past records and their institutions, and the larger numbers of applicants that are available from which to select. Even though the European students may have better academic records than the usual American student, the number of them who are "below average" needs explanation in view of what is presumably more critical screening. Possibly, European students may be admitted who cannot measure up to home standards; or they may be located in institutions in this country whose performance requirements are the most rigorous. It may be that less leniency in grading is evinced toward European students than toward more "exotic" students.

In any event, the difficulty of an objective study of foreign students' academic records raises as many questions as it resolves. Only when we have some comparison with a carefully matched American control group will it be possible to know whether the frequently voiced faculty complaints about the "quality" of foreign students are really valid.

Certificates

Whatever the objective evidence of academic achievement, the sense of personal accomplishment felt by foreign students in their academic studies in this country may have equal or even greater importance. This raises the question of certificates for foreign students who have had a constructive learning experience but who may not have completed work for a degree. This is a subject on which there is a wide variety of both opinion and practice. Most foreign student advisers recognize the personal and professional importance attached by many nationals to some more or less "honorific" statement of their educational experience in this country. The informal photostatic transcript of record does not satisfy the desire for a "symbolic" document.

In some colleges and universities documents whose design resembles a diploma for a degree are given to foreign students. The explicit intention is to provide them with a statement that can be displayed. On other campuses a less pretentious document serves the purpose. In many other institutions no concessions are made to the desire of foreign students for formal recognition of nondegree work. Those who defend the award of pretentious documents generally place primary value on satisfying the aspirations of individual foreign students in the interest of painless interpersonal relations with them. They point to the European custom of issuing certificates for a variety of minor educational activities and play down the possibility or the importance of having such documents misused or misinterpreted in other countries. However, the proponents of certificates as a rule do not advocate their being cheapened and would not have them presented to those who have frankly loafed through their work. There is no intention of providing foreign students with a second-class degree. Those who oppose the issuance of such certificates generally place primary value on some "absolute" standard of academic achievement and the reputation of American education abroad. It is also the feeling of these persons that certificates tend to detract from the satisfaction of those who have earned full degrees. Whatever virtues may attach to one or another of various positions on this issue, there would be considerable value in a certain uniformity of practice. The Association of American Universities or some comparable group should address itself to this subject. It is not a matter which foreign student advisers can resolve.

Administrative Support of Foreign Students on American Campuses

The presence of foreign students on American campuses has raised considerations ranging from the broad values inherent in the American educational system to the minutiae of evaluating foreign credits. One of the greatest contributions made by our foreign guests to academic institutions *qua* institutions may be precisely in the kind of self-scrutiny their presence has stimulated among the more thoughtful administrators and educators.

On the other hand, the administrative aid given to foreign students by American educational institutions has also been impressive. The following statement was inserted in the record of a Senate subcommittee hearing in reply to queries by Senator Fulbright on university cooperation in foreign student programs.

(1) Institutions of higher learning in the United States annually provide partial or full maintenance for approximately three-fourths of the foreign nationals who are studying in this country and financial support for more than one-half of the research scholars and visiting lecturers under the program administered by the Department (of State).

(2) Faculty members on more than 1,000 American campuses serve voluntarily as Fulbright program advisers and are assisted by committees established by the colleges for the preliminary screening of American student applicants. . . .

(3) Approximately 1,000 American universities have appointed foreign student advisers. . . .

(4) Faculty members of 62 American universities voluntarily serve on 47 selection committees . . . for lecturing and research awards.

(5) Continuing hospitality is offered . . . to all types of foreign grantees. . . .[12]

Saturation Points.—This list of the demands that international study places on educational institutions and their faculties is particularly impressive when one considers the heavy teaching

---

[12] U.S. Congress, Senate, *Overseas Information Programs of the United States*, 82nd Cong., 2nd Sess., Nov. 20-21, 1952 (Washington: Government Printing Office, 1953), p. 183.

and committee load already carried by most faculty members in the majority of institutions. It is equally impressive when one considers the varied and legitimate demands placed on limited university budgets.

It is not astonishing therefore that opinions have been voiced against any enlargement of the foreign student load by many faculty members. The complaints, when they occur, however, seem leveled primarily not at the load of normally enrolled foreign students but rather at the temporary visitors who may arrive on short notice, who may not arrive on schedule, or who may not arrive at all after preparations have been made to receive them. Other than the demand on time, there is also the financial drain that unavoidable hospitality entails. If the sources of these complaints are really with the visitor programs rather than with the regularly enrolled students, it would appear that the difficulty lies in part with the resource lists used by centralized program planners and the attraction exercised by distinguished personalities and institutions not only on planners but perhaps more importantly on the visitors themselves.

When one examines the question of the regularly enrolled foreign students, even the institutions with the largest percentage of foreign students do not appear overburdened compared to European institutions (see pages 28–30, and Appendix A). Therefore, from various college administrators, in contrast to the teaching staff, one hears expressed most frequently the desire for more foreign students. Only a few of the graduate and internationally known institutions voice the viewpoint that their institution cannot absorb additional numbers of foreign students. [13] Generally, the smaller, more remote, or less-developed undergraduate schools seem to want more foreign students than they can get. Occasionally, this may reflect a financial concern. To hard-pressed administrators foreign students may appear as another source of enrollment fees. This is

[13] For details see Appendix D.

not necessarily an illegitimate position, but it does not *per se* recommend the institutions. With the expected influx of American students which is now beginning, this situation will change radically and perhaps the change will be to the disadvantage of foreign applicants.

Least desirable are those rare proprietary schools that deliberately recruit foreign students for the financial returns they entail. Usually such schools do not possess the most desirable academic standards and their exploitive intent rarely escapes the notice of foreign students or reputable placement officers. At best, they may provide a steppingstone to better schools for academically able and economically self-sustaining students whose secondary training was inadequate. Naturally, information on the philosophy and practices of this marginal group of schools is not easily obtained. It does appear, however, that students from Latin-American and African countries are most frequently the targets of such institutions.

The opposite viewpoint of certain institutions that a saturation point in foreign students has been reached may reflect a series of managerial and educational problems. If the institution provides the foreign student with particular and concerned counseling, if its laboratories and other facilities are already heavily burdened, if educational privileges are granted, if personal relations are encouraged between students and teaching staff, and if nonnationals are treated as a "special problem," then undoubtedly the additional time and expense involved may tax an institution and its staff. Administratively, the additional burden of admission procedures, wise academic counseling, and governmental regulations and reports cannot be escaped. Nor is the appointment of a foreign student adviser with either direct additional cost to a university budget or indirect cost through loss of teaching time the sole answer.

There are a certain number of educational institutions in which there is general agreement that they have reached a saturation point in foreign student enrollment. Some institutions have an explicit 10 percent quota for foreign students. Others have a tacit quota policy. Some state-supported institutions feel that even the discussion of a quota might arouse certain elements in state legislatures to oppose the spending of any state funds for the education of foreigners. Given the great heterogeneity of American educational institutions, it is clear that no generalization is possible on what constitutes saturation and wise policies toward it. However, for the country as a whole and in purely quantitative terms, the number of foreign students in the United States cannot be considered at a saturation point with the possible exception of certain technical or professional schools, such as those in medicine. This appears to be true, particularly in view of the services generally accorded our own students and of additional services we feel called upon to give students from abroad. It is possible, however, that from the point of view of high quality (for example, good placement, work appropriate to the student, and so forth), the capacity to absorb more foreign students is not so great as our large and diffuse educational resources might at first imply.

For any particular institution, a saturation point is a function of its educational philosophy in general, of its counseling policies in particular, of the demands made by external agencies—such as the Department of State and its agents, like the Institute of International Education—of its financial resources, of its size and location, of the level of its teaching, and of a dozen other factors particular to each institution. Every institution would have to scrutinize its own situation with objectivity and integrity to reach any judicious conclusions on this score. It would have to consider the needs of foreign students as seriously as it considers its own self-interests. The mere willingness to accept foreign students does not necessarily assure an institution's capacity to handle them competently.

Affiliation

The capacity of an educational institution to provide foreign students with competent and relevant educational experience leads into another frequently debated subject, namely, "affiliation." Affiliation is the term generally used for a more or less intimate exchange relationship between an American college and a foreign counterpart. It is a term generally deemed to be less condescending than "adoption" and to represent in fact also a mutuality and reciprocity not generally implied by the word "adoption."

Closely allied to formal affiliation between American and foreign institutions is the question of deliberate or accidental specializations in certain regional or national groups. The arguments most frequently marshaled in favor of affiliation and to a lesser degree in favor of regional or national specializations are as follows.

First, a faculty that has a competent grasp of the conditions and problems of another area can usually teach the students from that area in terms that are more meaningful and relevant. For example, if the students are accustomed to theoretical rather than practical teaching, laboratory work can be especially designed to compensate for the lack of earlier training in manual dexterity and mechanical skills. Second, a prolonged interest in and knowledge of a given country generally facilitates warmer and more intimate personal contacts between American and foreign personnel. Third, as knowledge develops in the American institution of conditions in a particular country, more reliable selection is possible both because returned graduates can assist in the selection abroad and because personal judgments are possible concerning the reliability of overseas sponsors. Fourth, and for the same reasons, accreditation is facilitated and more accurately achieved. Fifth, upon return, a group of graduates from the same American institution will have common ties, can more easily understand each other, and will presumably have greater influence in their home country.

Those who argue against affiliation or regional specialization raise the following points: First, on large campuses or in big departments the great variety of area interests represented in the faculty neither should nor could appropriately be restricted or channeled. Second, on small campuses concentration on one or two national groups deprives these nationals as well as American students of the advantages of a broad international atmosphere. Third, national concentrations foster national cliques and reduce the opportunities for contact with American life. Fourth, in small American communities concentrations of particular national groups may give rise to negative reactions and the creation of prejudiced judgments.

These various viewpoints suggest that affiliation may be advantageous for certain professional and technical schools such as those in medicine or agriculture within large universities; that affiliations are usually possible, if at all, only between quite limited segments of graduate faculties in the social disciplines and the humanities; that affiliation for such faculties is probably most advantageous if there is a pre-existing area program for both research and teaching such as Cornell's Southeast Asia program; and that regional specialization or affiliation in general is unwanted and undesirable for undergraduate institutions of whatever size and for isolated professional and technical schools.

Predeparture Briefing

A final topic may deserve mention in a general consideration of policies and practices respecting foreign students on American campuses. This is the subject variously called predeparture briefing, debriefing, or reorientation. It is a subject in which there is a new and growing interest in the foreign student field but which has a longer and more entrenched role in the trainee and leader-technician field. If the postulated predeparture phase of adjustment is valid, then it would appear that the period of preparation for return to the homeland is indeed a crucial and sensitive one for many individuals. In the experiments so far carried out along these lines varying philosophies have either implicitly or explicitly prevailed.

In some instances stress has been laid on preparing students to consider clearly and practically the roles they may anticipate assuming on their return. The experiment at William and Mary College in 1953, where a group of ten French normal school students were given a week to consider their future activities back in France and where discussions were held primarily in French, belongs to this category. The intent was predominantly reorientation to France.

In other cases brief exit interviews are held on an individual or small-group basis in order to solicit frank and constructive opinions about the experiences encountered during the sojourn in the United States. The intent primarily is to evaluate the planning and execution of a program. In a sense this type of terminal interviewing can be designated as debriefing or as evaluation.

In still other cases the intent of terminal sessions, whether in groups or individually, is to provide an opportunity for foreign students to reappraise and to digest the American experience. Inevitably, certain individuals leave the United States with distressing or puzzling questions still rankling in their minds. A final opportunity to bring them to light and discuss them frankly, particularly with fellow-foreign students or fellow-nationals, is considered constructive.

Lastly, there are some individuals who view terminal services and opportunities in terms of a final gesture of courtesy and good will to students, some of whom may be leaving this country with a sense of being sent rather unceremoniously on their way.

Of course, no watertight line can be drawn between the

various intentions that underlie the different kinds of terminal sessions. Nor is there any convincing research evidence bearing on the effectiveness of various procedures in relation to various intentions. Nor is there any particularly cogent argument for educational institutions undertaking obligations in these directions beyond the sense of good will toward our foreign guests that is prevalent in this country. Nevertheless, an important aspect is that almost any kind of well-conducted terminal session can be educational in a cognitive and in an emotional sense. Insightful leaders of such conferences should be able to effect a considerable degree of superficial therapy for individuals who may need it. It might also be argued that, since the sojourn abroad is merely an episode in a total learning experience, any educational device that attempts to summarize and take stock is appropriate for both American and overseas participants. It will behoove American educational institutions to follow closely the experimental efforts being made by certain pioneer groups in this direction.

It should be stressed finally that the reactions to the American sojourn expressed during the predeparture period will not necessarily dominate recall of the sojourn once the individual has reached home. Predeparture affect is no more indicative of the total influence of the sojourn experience than is affect during the spectator phase in determining the reactions of a student throughout his stay in the host country.

Conclusions

No attempt will be made to recapitulate the content of this chapter on policies and practices with respect to foreign students on American campuses. Each topic is clearly captioned in the text and is already only a summary of subjects that are frequently discussed at much greater length by interested educational administrators, counselors, and teaching staff. On most topics the wide range of existing views has been briefly sketched and whenever possible the supporting arguments for one or another view have been marshaled. Frequently the differences in policies and practices are attributable to situational factors peculiar to different institutions.

Several general conclusions emerge from this rapid survey. First, each campus must develop policies and practices with respect to foreign students based not only on its local institutional situation but also on a broad knowledge of foreign student programs and of foreign students as socially and psychologically determined individuals who have varying needs. Every educational institution is not equally prepared to satisfy programmatic goals or individual needs.

Second, each institution has an obligation to make a full and explicit statement of its policies and practices in respect to foreign students. Only in this fashion can the heterogeneous but interlocking interests of American colleges and universities, individual foreign students, and program administrators be best served. The campus study committees under the Carnegie Endowment for International Peace program on Universities and World Affairs have in some instances provided a first step in this direction.

Third, certain needs exist for constructive leadership and for fact-finding that extend beyond individual campuses and might be undertaken by one or another of the associations of professional groups. Among such undertakings can be listed: (1) a revision of the *Handbook for Counselors of Students from Abroad;* (2) development of relations with cultural and educational attachés, both those from abroad and those serving the United States in foreign countries; (3) studies of most advantageous housing facilities for foreign students; (4) centralized, current, and accurate information on accreditation; (5) certificates for students who have not completed work for a degree; (6) a guide to the capacity of different types of institutions to absorb foreign students; (7) a review of experience to date on affiliation between American and foreign institutions with suggestions for the best practices in such relationships; and (8) study of predeparture briefing of various types.

Although suggestions of this specific nature are made only in the context of the final chapter of this volume, any review of the relationship of foreign students and higher education in the United States must reveal the need for continuity of experience, for new and meaningfully collected data, and for constant reappraisal of practices if we in the United States are to offer students from abroad constructive educational opportunities.

Appendixes

Appendix A

Twenty-Five U. S. Institutions Having the Largest Foreign Student Enrollment in 1951-52

Institution	Number of Foreign Students	Total Enrollment Resident Students	Percentage Foreign Students to Total Student Enrollment	Rank of Institution in Percentage of Foreign Students
1. University of California	1,459	34,883	4.2	8
2. Columbia University	1,379	27,278	5.1	5
3. New York University	1,185	45,186	2.6	17
4. University of Michigan	781	17,035	4.6	7
5. Harvard University	730	10,239	7.1	3
6. University of Minnesota	512	18,682	2.7	16
7. Massachusetts Institute of Technology	493	4,874	10.1	2
8. University of Washington	449	13,297	3.4	12
9. University of Wisconsin	423	16,142	2.6	18
10. University of Illinois	417	20,105	2.1	20
11. Cornell University	400	9,926	4.0	9
12. University of Chicago	355	7,431	4.8	6
13. Montezuma Seminary	355	355	100.0	1
14. University of Southern California	303	10,857	2.8	14
15. University of Texas	303	12,290	2.5	19
16. University of Pennsylvania	295	16,299	1.8	22
17. Stanford University	271	7,584	3.6	11
18. George Washington University	259	9,541	2.7	15
19. Syracuse University	257	14,459	1.8	23
20. Louisiana State University	256	6,608	3.9	10
21. Michigan State College	247	13,417	1.8	21
22. Yale University	247	7,270	3.4	13
23. Indiana University	231	17,578	1.3	24
24. Ohio State University	213	18,482	1.2	25
25. Howard University	212	3,697	5.7	4

Total.... 12,032 (39.5 percent of total foreign student enrollment)

Source: Institute of International Education, *Education for One World, 1951–52* (New York: The Institute, 1952), p. 20.

Appendix B

Country	1930–31	1951–52	Country	1930–31	1951–52
Afghanistan	1	79	Korea	124	288
Argentina	33	196	Lebanon		147
Australia	41	177	Liberia	1	99
Austria	66	233	Luxembourg		8
Belgium	19	144	Malaya	6	157
Bolivia	32	192	Mexico	325	1,176
Brazil	36	471	Netherlands	63	385
British West Indies	159	54	New Zealand	18	72
Burma	2	90	Nicaragua	22	151
Canada	1,313	4,193	Nigeria		226
Chile	36	161	Norway	79	409
China	1,306	2,918	Pakistan		187
Colombia	70	952	Panama	111	356
Costa Rica	35	147	Paraguay	2	32
Cuba	150	675	Peru	47	259
Denmark	51	128	Philippine Islands	890	880
Dominican Republic	5	95	Portugal	6	59
Ecuador	14	127	Saudi Arabia	7	17
Egypt	35	344	Sierra Leone		43
El Salvador	8	142	Spain	61	142
Ethiopia		41	Sweden	69	223
Finland	30	144	Switzerland	95	189
France	143	588	Syria	52	124
Germany	415	1,234	Thailand	27	268
Gold Coast		66	Turkey	117	417
Greece	99	651	Union of So. Africa	72	95
Guatemala	15	182	United Kingdom	615	1,054
Haiti	10	78	Uruguay	2	49
Honduras	24	116	Venezuela	26	447
Iceland	3	42	Yugoslavia	20	80
India	195	1,099	Stateless		121
Indonesia	5	130	Undesignated		553
Iran	41	859	All others	1,048	1,924
Iraq	11	499			
Ireland	86	101	Total	9,643	30,462
Israel		779			
Italy	170	386			
Japan	987	1,133			
Jordan and Palestine	92	179			

Source; This material is extracted from Institute of International Education, *Education for One World, 1951–52* (New York: The Institute, 1952), pp. 45–46.

Appendix C

| Suggestions Made in 1925
for Assisting Foreign Students
in the United States [1]

THE FOLLOWING suggestions are a highly condensed summary of chapter 9 in *The Foreign Student in America.*

1. Students should not study in the United States while they are still immature; graduates rather than undergraduates are preferable. This was stressed especially for China, Latin America, and the Near East.
2. Teaching should stress practice rather than theory. This was brought out especially with respect to China.
3. Scholarships should be granted with the understanding that recipients must return home. This was stressed for the Near East.
4. The importance of personal relationships for all students was stressed—friends, "mothers," families, etc., by most discussants.
5. Responsibility for welfare of foreign students was variously placed on individual institutions, churches or other Christian organizations, communities, and on the government of the United States (one discussant).
6. Foreign governments should appoint a representative to care for students of their nationality.
7. Colleges should have foreign student counselors.
8. Organizations of national groups on campuses should be encouraged. This was stressed for Philippine students.
9. The American people should be educated about foreign countries.
10. Returned foreign students should be urged to organize "alumni" in their homelands.

[1] W. R. Wheeler, H. H. King, and A. B. Davidson (eds.), *The Foreign Student in America* (New York: Association Press, 1925).

Appendix D

Views on Capacity of American
Educational Institutions to
Absorb More Foreign Students [1]

IN REPLY to the question:

"Do you believe that our universities have enough room for the
absorption of additional foreign students at the graduate and
undergraduate levels, under the program as presently conducted?"

Answers were tabulated as follows:

Reply	Number	Percent
Yes—without comment	97	50
Yes—particularly for small colleges and universities....	9	5
Yes—with reservations	65	34
No—without comment	4	2
No comment, don't know	18	9
Total	193	100

Eighty-nine per cent of the administrators replying to the question
felt that at least for the present and immediate future this absorption
can be accomplished. Fifty per cent of the respondents offered an
unqualified [2] affirmative answer to the query, while another five
per cent thought that small colleges in particular could enroll more
exchangees:

[1] Bureau of Social Science Research, American University, *The Student
Exchange Program: An Appraisal by 193 Educators and 77 Business and
Organization Executives*, prepared for International Evaluation Staff, IIA,
Dept. of State, January 1953, pp. 24–26.
[2] *Author's note:* Without access to the original material, it is not possible
to know whether replies meant unqualified approval or simply whether a
questionnaire was checked and no comments were inserted.

The larger universities have approximately three per cent of their enrollment in foreign students. Smaller colleges have less than one-half of one per cent. A widespread distribution of foreign students in all universities and colleges would accomplish the purpose of better acquaintance with American life and culture as it is lived not only in large cities but in small towns and rural areas of our land. [Concordia College]

Thirty-four per cent qualified an affirmative reply in some fashion. The largest number of these—thirteen per cent of all respondents—felt that additional funds would be needed for expansion:

I believe that our universities and colleges can absorb many more foreign students at both graduate and undergraduate levels under the present program, provided of course that the financing of educational exchanges does not fall on the already overburdened budgets of the universities. [University of Kansas]

Six per cent of the respondents thought that colleges could continue to admit additional exchange students for a limited time, as did this official of a small liberal arts college:

From information gained, I should say that during the next two years at least the colleges would have room for the absorption of additional foreign students. [Shorter College]

Five per cent of the university administrators responding felt that certain changes in the exchange program, as it is presently run, would have to be initiated before their schools could take on additional foreign students. The two changes suggested here were more careful selection and screening of exchange students as well as a more coordinated approach to the administration of the present exchange program.

We could take more students and would be glad to have them if they came properly screened and qualified. We have discovered that many students inform our consuls abroad that they have sufficient funds to take care of the academic year. This turns out not to be the case. . . . [Ohio University]

The remaining respondents who offered qualified "yes" to the question of whether colleges could absorb additional exchange students either:

a) pointed out the need for increased personnel and facilities (4 per cent);

b) indicated that only limited numbers could be absorbed (4 per cent);

c) suggested that such professional institutions as law and medical schools could not handle additional foreign students (2 per cent).

Two per cent of the university officials queried suggested that American institutions of higher learning could not absorb more student exchangees.

One-tenth of the sample did not answer the question.

Appendix E

Analysis of Institute of
International Education Staffing
for 1930 and 1952 [1]

In 1930, 20 persons were concerned in the Institute of International
Education student program, either directly or in an executive capacity,
although there was a total staff of 25 people. At that time, IIE-related
students numbered 361, of whom 191 were outbound Americans
and 170 were inbound foreign students. This represented about 1.8
percent of the total foreign student population of 9,961 at that date.
The student program staff of 20 carried an average per capita load
of 18 students.

In 1952 the Institute of International Education had a permanent
staff of 110 persons in the United States and foreign student program,
15 executives, secretaries, a greatly enlarged accounting department
and a total staff of about 228 persons. In that year, IIE-related
students numbered 4,241 of whom 1,087 were outbound Americans
and 3,154 were inbound foreign students or specialists. This represented about 13 percent of the total foreign student population of
30,462 at that date. Within IIE, the staff of over 110 persons carried
an average per capita load of 30 students.

[1] The writer is indebted to Mrs. Vandi Haygood for the material included here.

Appendix F

Statement on the Language
Problem of Foreign Students [1]

IN THE QUESTIONNAIRE that was sent out for the collection of data
on foreign-student performance, the universities were asked to give
information, if available, on the English language difficulties of
individual students and the effect upon their work. It developed that
very few schools were able to furnish such information. Your Committee then decided that it would be desirable to find out what the
practice was among Association members in the matter of testing the
English competence of foreign students and offering special instruction
for those whose English proved to be deficient. Accordingly, last
July, a questionnaire was sent to each member school, and replies
were received from 34. Twenty-one of these schools give no English
examination to foreign students, either upon or before entrance to the
Graduate School. Nine give such examinations to all entering foreign
students, and four give them only to students referred by the departments or by advisors as showing deficiency in the language.

The degree of competence in English, as indicated by the
examinations, determines whether a student will be required to take
special work in English. In eleven schools, English courses for
foreign students are offered in the English Department; in four,
full-time work is offered in a special program; in six, courses are
offered in departments other than English, such as Speech or Linguistics; in five, help is provided through individual aid or tutoring; one
school sends students to a nearby college. From these data, it is
clear that about one-half of the members of the Association regard

[1] An excerpt from a report in "Journal of Proceedings and Addresses of
the Fifty-fourth Annual Conference of the Association of American Universities and Fifth Annual Conference of the Association of Graduate
Schools," Oct. 12, 1953 (Mimeographed).

the English ability of students as a problem requiring attention. North Carolina, the Massachusetts Institute of Technology, and Princeton, however, reported very little trouble in this regard because of care in the selection of students. This fall, for the first time, Harvard has offered a four-week orientation course for foreign students preceding the opening of the school year; special emphasis is put on training in English.

Last year, a preliminary report was made on objective tests of a foreign student's proficiency in the use of English that had been developed by Professor Robert Lado, of the English Language Institute of the University of Michigan. Since that time, considerable experience has been gained from further use of these tests. During the past year, the English language test was used by the Department of State in selecting scholarship candidates from Japan. More than 2,000 candidates were examined, and the field office reported complete satisfaction with the results and is planning to use the test again in Japan next year. In the summer of 1952, this same test had been taken by 100 German students who were brought to this country for an orientation program. It was given to them at the beginning and at the end of the orientation period and the papers were graded in the State Department offices that administered it. The test scores and the subjective evaluation of the students' proficiency by their instructors showed a close correlation. For over a year, a similar objective test developed by Dr. Lado has been given in several binational centers sponsored by the Department of State in Greece and in a number of Latin-American countries. In this case, the papers were sent to the English Language Institute of the University of Michigan for evaluation and for certification of the student's proficiency in English. Although the students were charged a fee of $5.00 in United States money for the privilege of taking the test, more than 600 took it—an indication of the need and interest felt in foreign countries.

The test can be given at low cost, however, as in the Japanese program where the State Department printed, administered, and scored them. They do not require individual administration, and can be supervised and graded by the clerical staff. Their validity and accuracy seem to be well established. It would be a great step forward if the State Department could arrange to have these or similar tests administered by Cultural Offices and consular officials throughout the world, and so practically eliminate, in their own countries, those students whose language difficulties will be a serious handicap after they get here. At the present time, these officials depend on statements of student proficiency from teachers, on conversations with the students, or upon a subjective test that requires individual administration and judgment of the student's answers. The results of this sort of testing are highly variable and often unsatisfactory. The most distressing cases of students with language deficiency who have entered our graduate schools have received consular approval of their English competence.

Index

INDEX

Studies in
Universities and
World Affairs